"This book is a must read not just for the victims of abuse but for those who care for them. It puts a real face to the statistics and "book learning." If a beautiful, bright articulate woman can get caught up in this horror, it could also be your client, your neighbor, your sister...yourself. Read it for your professional growth, read it to save someone you love."
Dr. Diane Marshall-Morgan
Psychologist and Author

"A Worthy Woman is indispensable for healthcare professionals as first points of contact for many victims. The knowledge gained from this book will inspire heightened awareness and compassion, ultimately saving lives."
Cheryl B. Siegwald-Mays, RN, MBA
Director of Mental Health at a Metropolitan hospital.

"A truthful, touching story written by a psychologist herself. The self-help is based in real life. Not to be missed!"
Dr. Mary Franzen Clark
Hiding Hurting Healing

A Worthy Woman

Victory Over Domestic Violence
A True Story and Self-Help Book

by
Dr. Gail Majcher

PublishAmerica
Baltimore

© 2000 by Dr. Gail Majcher.

First printing

ISBN: 1-59129-596-3
PUBLISHED BY PUBLISHAMERICA BOOK PUBLISHERS
www.publishamerica.com
Baltimore

Printed in the United States of America

To
Danialle and Joshua
who have been the joy of my life
And my Mother
who gave me life

Acknowledgements:

For their help in making <u>A Worthy Woman</u> a reality I would like to thank the following:

God, my inspiration for living.

Julius Passeri, my dear husband, who made many latte runs and never complained when I was huddled over the computer for days on end.

Danialle and Joshua, my children, who understood and supported my need to write this book even though it meant public exposure to our private lives.

Cheryl Mays, for being my best friend, spiritual sister and laughing partner.

My mother, now passed on but never forgotten.

Patricia Hoth, my first therapist, for seeing something worthy in me.

Andrew Hamilton, my literary agent, for understanding the need to have this book published.

All the wonderful people who live and work at the domestic violence shelters. May God bless you.

The makers of delicious chocolate goodies that kept me happy during this book writing process.

Contents

The Children

INTRODUCTION

"Why didn't I know this was happening to you?"

After reading my manuscript my mother wept as she realized what I had gone through. I was stunned. Had I not fled to her home with my babies on several occasions, bruised and battered? Yet her reaction is typical. Family members and friends find it hard to comprehend that domestic violence, beatings, and battering really happen in the home of a "normal" couple. Certainly, violence could not possibly be occurring in the quiet, suburban homes of people we associate with. But it does. I know because it happened to me.

This is a true story. It is about how my life was affected by domestic violence and what I have learned through this experience. Today I am a clinical psychologist, back then I was a naive, young girl who made a poor choice. Through my many years of training and by counseling hundreds of abused women, I have gained an understanding of what happened to me so many years ago. In hopes that it may bring domestic violence out from the shadows in society, I'm going to tell you of my horrifying experience as an abused wife and, fortunately, of my escape and the successful life that followed

Whether it is a blessing or curse, I've endured many challenging experiences in my relatively short journey through life. Many of my fellow baby boomers will be able to relate to the problems I have encountered, for the issues are pervasive amongst our generation. Despite being weaned on Ozzie and Harriet, many of us boomers have not had an ideal life. Dysfunctional families, drugs, unplanned pregnancy, domestic violence, addiction, divorce, welfare, single parenting, and remarriage are all part of our collective life. We have all been there, done that. Life certainly turned out differently than I had envisioned when I was a winsome flower child wearing love beads and preaching the virtues of peace

All these issues play a role in my story about experiencing

and overcoming the terrible tragedy of spousal abuse. Somehow, I never thought domestic violence would be a part of my life's story but it was. Fortunately, I made it out alive. I even remained sane no matter how desperate things appeared. Believe me, I know desperate. Desperate and I are much better acquainted than I would wish for anyone. But in spite of the pain from the abuse, I am convinced we are created as spiritual beings that can rise above circumstances and move on to find joy and peace. I have had my share of testing this theory as a battered wife, sometimes victorious and sometimes not.

It has been more than twenty years since I was physically and mentally abused by my spouse, yet I realize that the deep rooted scars will never fully heal. Recently I spoke to a group of abused women at a shelter. I discussed my experience as a young battered wife, my escape and the road to success that followed. On my way home I found myself crying in the car because the sadness of their stories mirrored my own. While working with abused women I have come to realize our stories are very similar. In many ways, my story is every victim's story. Different names and faces, the same terrible experiences.

Like many abused women I believed if you loved someone enough, he or she would become a healthy, loving individual capable of loving you back. I thought my love could heal my husband's wounds. I was wrong. We do not have that much control over another person's will. I learned the hard way I could love my spouse until the cows came home and that did not mean he would ever be capable of loving me in return. My spouse, like most abusers, was not capable of feeling genuine empathy or compassion for me because he was consumed by his own inner turmoil. And I learned with time that I had no control over his violence. He was who he was. I could not "fix" him. In retrospect, I realize I was trying to control my husband through enabling love just as he was trying to control me through violence. Neither approach worked.

Abusers feel "object love" for their partners. Spouses are viewed as objects to be used for their need fulfillment not as feeling, thinking human beings. That is why abuse is acceptable to them. I made many excuses for my spouse's behavior and so did others, but there is NO excuse for abuse. Excusing the violence does not help anyone. The way to stop this terrible crime of domestic violence is for the abusers to assume one hundred percent responsibility for their behavior and for the victims to develop zero tolerance for the abuse. This is easier said then done.

There are three primary reasons for telling my tale. First, there is a desperate need in our society for the public to understand domestic violence. This is a true story. Understanding my story is a giant step in understanding every abused woman's story. The journal I kept during the end of my marriage is the heart and soul of the first part of the book. My psychological and spiritual knowledge is the body, which encases it. As a psychologist I have had the opportunity to understand the elements in my life that led me to being the type of person who would get into an abusive situation and, also, be able to get out.

Second, there is a need for people to know that domestic violence can be overcome. Stopping the violence in our society must begin in the home. The second part of this book is a definitive self-help section for anyone associated with domestic violence. The focus is on the victim, the abuser and the children. It has very specific advice on how the victim can get safe and stay safe. The question of "why the abuser abuses" is addressed as well as what can be done to stop his violence. The last two chapters are concerned with the children; who are the overlooked victims. An effective four step method of disciplining children without violence is discussed.

Third, society must believe that a woman can escape the abuse and go on to create a good life for herself and her children even when it seems hopeless. If I could do it, so can you. I promised myself many years ago I would tell my story to help other victims if I survived. And I did, thank you very much.

There is much to be said for difficult life experiences. Hopefully, we grow in strength and wisdom as we overcome the challenges. I have often said in retrospect, I am ever so grateful for my education; but I realize the primary substance of my being an effective psychologist is my own life experiences. In one way or another I have walked in every person's shoes that has come into my office. I understand their pain and their feelings because I have also felt them in my life. I am thankful for this empathy that came through life's trials.

By the grace of God, I have been able to grow and successfully make it out of a violent marriage, though not without a great deal of suffering and anguish. But when all was said and done I have moved forward a few notches in this game of life. This is what I want for you.

Perhaps you will be able to identify with something I have gone through. Or maybe this book will make you grateful for the ease of your own struggles. Whatever your reaction is to my story I hope that somehow, in some way, you grow as a person. But even more so, I hope you develop a greater understanding and compassion for what domestic violence is all about.

If you are currently in a violent situation, let the information in this book help you to get safe. You do have the option of getting out. It is possible. You are a victim, but that does not mean that you have no power. I know because I did it, against all odds. You and your children can have a healthy, successful life. Read on.

Part One: My Story
The Past

Chapter One: Domestic Violence

Domestic violence.......Spousal abuse.......Battered women Easy words to pass right by UNLESS you or someone you love has experienced the horror of violence. Every story told still causes a flood of emotions to emerge from deep within my soul because I remember the hell of that existence like it was yesterday. I forgave my ex-husband years ago but the scars within me will never go away. They are etched in my psyche forever. At times I still weep for that young girl who was living in such pain. I also weep for those still in the pain and I weep the most for those who do not survive. There is a thin line between a beating and a murder. Let me repeat, there is a thin line between a beating and a murder. It is only varying degrees of the same violence.

I knew, without a shadow of a doubt, my former husband had it within him to kill me. When he was out of control there were no internal boundaries on his behavior and I never knew how far he would take the abuse. I often wondered if this would be the time he would finally do it. After I left, I kept looking over my shoulder to make sure I was safe. Escaping does not guarantee that the violence is over.

THE TRIAL OF THE CENTURY

My heart breaks for Nicole Brown Simpson. I understand why she stayed in the alleged abusive relationship. Anyone who has been there understands how the insanity damages the self-esteem. The sense of self becomes so disturbed that one stays, too weak to oppose the abuser and too frightened to face reality. I understand her and I understand the attacker and it makes my skin crawl.

I had no intention of watching "the trial of the century" on television but, like many Americans, I found a compulsion to turn it on whenever possible. I could not take my eyes off of O.J.'s face. Because there, within his eyes, I saw the same emptiness that existed in my spouse's eyes when he was violent. It fascinated me and sickened me. There was something much too familiar about the look in this man's eyes. I did not need to hear the details about the case, seeing the emptiness was enough for me to know the truth. I have seen the same look in the eyes of people I have counseled who have been violent. Any person who has ever been abused in any way knows that look.

Emotions long buried were stirred up inside me. Nicole and I were one in our shared experience of abuse. This trial was about her and about me and about every other woman who ever experienced the horror of abuse. The day the verdict was announced I had come home at lunch from work to pick up something. As I ran up the stairs I heard the jury announce the verdict. I sat down and just starting crying. I was surprised by the intensity of my own reaction. Then I realized I was crying for all of us who have been so unfairly treated as a result of domestic violence. Where is the justice? Where was the hope? I knew then I had to write my story because, unlike Nicole Brown Simpson's, it has a happy ending. My children did not lose their mother.

For those who do not know the faces of abuse, they are not

all like the unhealthy people you see on the raunchy talk shows. Domestic violence happens to women from all walks of life. Rich, poor, black, white, educated, uneducated; we are all in this together. The epidemic of this crime extends to all socioeconomic levels and races.

THE SAD STATISTICS

It is important to know the incredible statistics on domestic violence. Approximately every 18 seconds in the United States a woman is beaten by her significant other. According to the U.S. Department of Justice, it is reported that husbands or boyfriends batter more than a million women a year. The number is even greater with the unreported incidences. One out of four women will be in an abusive relationship in her lifetime. One third of these assaults involve a weapon and the abuser has also raped 40 percent of the victims. More than one half of the women murdered in our great country are killed by their spouse or lover. The very men who have promised to love and protect these women are killing them. Women are dying daily at the hands of their partners. Aren't these facts mind-boggling? I thought I was alone with this problem, but it holds millions of people captive.

I know what a nightmare being a victim of domestic violence is and I am so saddened to realize how many women are experiencing it day in and day out. Yet it is rarely discussed. Over twenty years ago I did research on domestic violence for the National Science Foundation and I am appalled to find that the current statistics have not changed in all of these years, in spite of how far women have come in other areas. We continue to close our eyes to the fact that women are being brutalized and murdered daily within the confines of their homes. We say that it is not our business.

What is wrong with our society that it accepts brutal assaults against its women?!! Men are getting away with murder. And no one is talking about it. Occasionally there will be frenzied reports in the mass media about domestic violence due to some sensational story. But then the interest dies out and we forget about the daily brutality that is occurring in every neighborhood in our country.

It horrifies and frightens me to realize how many people are being brutalized by this terrible crime; and the number is increasing. We need to share our life experiences in an effort to help one another and raise public awareness about domestic violence. Realizing that I was not alone in this terrible experience of domestic violence helped me accept that my spouse's violent behavior was something beyond my actions and me. His violence was not my fault and was not under my control. I kept trying to make sense of his behavior by examining my own to see what I had done wrong. I wanted it to make sense. I thought I must have been doing something wrong to warrant such treatment. It is very hard to make sense of violence when you are the victim and alone. Many women have thanked me for sharing my story because it is a replica of their own which helps them to feel sane. My story is their story.

UNANSWERED QUESTIONS

The most common questions I have been asked is "Why does SHE stay?" and "Why doesn't SHE just leave?" Most women leave at least eight times before finally making the escape or being murdered. I don't know how many times I escaped to my mother's home before the final break. Leaving a marriage with a broken down sense of self is an extremely difficult task to accomplish.

When will the questions become "What is HIS punishment?" "Where is HE being detained?" "Why should SHE and the children leave their home and their belongings?" "What can we do to help HER?" These questions I have rarely heard. Let's put the responsibility where it belongs; on his potentially homicidal behavior, not on her codependency.

"VICTIM"

More than twenty years ago when I was a victim of domestic violence I knew I would someday write a book about it if I survived. At the time the title became very clear to me. The book would be called <u>A Worthy Woman</u> because someone made me realize that I was, indeed, worthy. But, more on that later. What I did not realize was that I would need so many years of distancing from the abuse before I could bring myself to sit down and write about it. It takes a long time for the wounds to heal. Post traumatic stress is a very real phenomenon for many abused women who leave a violent relationship. Being a victim is like living in a nightmare that you think you cannot escape. But the good news is you can.

Although the world of psychology hesitates to use the word "victim," a woman who is being physically and mentally abused by her spouse does become a victim of his insanity. She is also a victim of society's chauvinistic attitude regarding domestic violence and, worst of all, she becomes a victim of her own damaged psyche. The self-esteem becomes buried under a mountain of doubts and fears. Even after ending the relationship, it takes a long time to overcome the emotional damage that is created by the abuse.

FACING THE LION

Fortunately I have learned through this experience that almost any painful obstacle can be overcome by moving forward emotionally. We can grow mentally and spiritually from any traumatic experience, even spousal abuse. But we cannot overcome anything until we face it. Staying in the marriage and denying the abuse as long as I did was an attempt to avoid the inevitable conflicts associated with the escape. I was afraid to face what I knew I would need to do.

One day during the abusive marriage I heard a speaker on television use the phrase "run to the roar" and it became very real to me. As humans we want to run in the opposite direction from the Lion but the only way to overcome him is by facing him. I did not want to, but I knew that I had to face the Lion of abuse. Closing my eyes to the violence never made it go away, it only increased in frequency and intensity.

At some point anyone associated with abuse needs to face the Lion by changing their own unhealthy patterns that allow it to happen. Old, destructive behavior patterns need to be replaced with new, healthier ones. We all know stories about people who get out of bad situations only to get right back into them. Different names and faces, but the same scenario. Many women leave one abusive situation only to end up in another one. The Lion returns until we conquer him by looking at ourselves. To this day I keep a stuffed lion in my office and my home. They remind me never to run from the roar, only towards it. I would like to think that sharing my story would set free what is left of my past Lions, and yours.

LIFTING THE RUG OF DENIAL

Now that domestic violence is finally coming out of the shadows and into the media spotlight, we must keep this topic at the conscious level of our society. We need to speak out and tell our stories. We need to keep having conversations about it. We cannot continue to keep sweeping it under the rug. Domestic violence is too big in our society; it no longer fits under the rug of denial. Too many lives are at stake. We must keep the dialogue going.

I hope you grow in compassion about domestic violence from reading about my experience. The Bible says "you will know the truth and the truth will set you free" (John 8:32). This book tells the truth about domestic violence. It is a true story.

As a society, we must stop closing our eyes to the spousal abuse. We must get out of denial to be set free from the grip violence has on us. Women are being beaten and dying daily at the hands of their partners; and few people are talking about it. Whether you are in an abusive relationship or not, you are impacted by domestic violence because it is spilling onto our streets onto our children.

I am one of the lucky ones who survived with my children and made a success of our lives in spite of the scars. I made the escape and went forward in life. If I could do it, so can you. I had nothing and I was alone with two small babies but survival meant leaving and worrying about that later. Today I am a clinical psychologist, back then I had no money, a limited education and very little support from those around me. I had to go on welfare to survive. But I did it. So can you. It was hard as hell, but easier than being abused.

And I am alive.

Chapter Two: Dancing for Nothing

So why does a woman stay? Why doesn't "she just leave?" Why did I stay? Our collective society lacks an understanding as to why a woman would get herself in a violent situation and why she stays. There are no clear-cut answers, but I can tell you the key elements of my background that led me to being an abused wife. Throughout my childhood I just naturally spent time analyzing the behavior of others. When someone was not acting "normal" I wanted to figure out why and make sense of it. Maybe it was my coping technique for feeling sane in a dysfunctional family. Needless to say, as a clinical psychologist and with my personality type I have spent years analyzing what happened in my life.

A BABY BOOM CHILDHOOD

Structurally my family was like many families of the baby boom era. My father worked long hours and was not home much. Our parents had come out of the depression and they truly knew what it was to struggle financially. Consequently, the most important parenting issue to them was making sure they had a roof over our heads and food on the table. A father's sole responsibility was to earn money; that was the norm. He did not have to worry about the home and the children because that was the woman's job.

People were not typically in touch with mental health back then. Terms like "dysfunctional family" and "emotional fulfillment" were not within our parents' verbal repertoire. Verbal, physical and sexual abuse were hidden and not talked about. "What will the neighbors think?" was a theme in my home as well as in most of my friends' homes. The appearance of being a happy family was all-important. The facade became more important than the reality.

Being a parent of adult children now, I can appreciate that our parents were doing the best they could with the knowledge they had. They provided materially for us because that's what they knew to do. Mental health was not an issue of concern nor was it thought about. My parents provided my two sisters and me with a lovely middle class home and most of the material possessions that we wanted. Emotional need fulfillment did not factor into the equation of a good home.

My mom was your "typical" mom from the '60s. Because of my mother I have many wonderful memories of vacations, birthday parties, holiday gatherings, ballet, Girl Scouts etc. She was a homemaker and no one; I mean no one, could out bake my mother. Baking was her forte. Store bought desserts were frowned upon. My mother was not really fulfilled in her homemaker role but women's choices were limited back then. She made the best of it by excelling in her homemaker duties. My childhood friends still comment about my mother's cooking.

My mother had to drop out of high school to help support the family and she was never able to fulfill her dreams of getting an education. My grandparents had money for the boys to go to college, but they thought it was a waste of money for a female to get an education. My mother was bright and would have been much happier with a career. I always knew she was depressed and emotionally unfulfilled.

DANCING AS FAST AS I COULD

I have spent most of my life trying to make my mother happy. When I was a child I thought if I were good enough, she would be happy. When I got older I thought if I accomplished enough and gave her wonderful life experiences, I would make her happy. My business associate, Babs, calls it "dancing as fast as you can." It took me years to realize and accept that I do not and never did have the power to make my mother happy. That was an issue within her. But my trying had a profound impact on my life choices. My abusive marriage is a prime example of repeating the pattern from childhood of "dancing as fast as I can" to make my husband healthy and happy. And I did try. I thought if I was the perfect wife and mother, he would be normal and nonviolent. Of course, I was wrong.

Oh my, how we have a tendency to repeat those imbedded patterns learned in childhood. In psychology, we call it the repetition compulsion. We have a compulsion to repeat the patterns from childhood, hoping for a different ending.

Like many couples, my parents had a troubled marriage by the time I was born. Marriage counseling and communication with feelings was not the norm back then. Yelling, throwing things and tension was much more common. I still cringe when I hear cupboard doors slam or people yelling. Fond memories. And like it or not, we are products of our childhood homes. We learn about relationships by observing our parents and by our attachments to them.

My father was very handsome and had a wonderful personality. He was also an emotionally detached alcoholic. When I was born, my father took one look at me and determined I was not his and proceeded to treat me that way throughout my life. He never held me on his lap or called me by my first name. There was no concrete evidence to my father's claim but it was a way to punish my mother for not being whom he thought she should be to make him happy. Alcoholics can be irrational and delusional. A blood test would have cleared up the issue but the emotional damage was already done.

My dad died in a car accident when I was eighteen as a result of his drinking and driving. It was too bad because I really needed a father at that time in my life. Actually, I always needed one. What's that song? "You can't always get what you want...but you get what you need.... "Although my father rejected me, I did benefit from his generosity, intelligence and fun personality by being one of "the girls." I have many fun memories of times spent with my sisters and him. With my father, I was also dancing as fast as I could in an attempt to get him to accept me. My life revolved around pleasing others. Is it surprising that I became a co-dependent and a victim of abuse?

SIBLING SUPPORT

Although I was popular in school and got many strokes from my male and female friends, deep inside I had a low self-esteem and was dying emotionally. This little girl, like all children, needed unconditional love and acceptance from her parents. I didn't have that but fortunately I had my close friends and my sisters. Janis is four years older than me. When we were children she tried to fulfill some of the parental voids from the family system. But she was just a child herself trying to assume an adult role.

Marcia is my other sister and only eighteen months older than me. While Janis was our idol and role model, Marcia was my buddy and pal. In childhood, we were very close and supportive of each other. Certainly one of the reasons I survived some of the traumas of childhood is that Janis, Marcia and I learned a wonderful form of coping from my father called laughter. We were able to deny and repress all kinds of painful experiences by finding humor in almost everything. We still do. It does not take much to get us going. Laughter is not a bad coping skill although, for us, it was out of balance. In many dysfunctional childhood homes siblings subconsciously unite and find ways of coping to survive emotional pain.

Am I blaming my parents for me ending up in a violent marriage? Absolutely not. I know my parents were doing the best they could. And God bless them, especially my mother, for all of the good they brought into my life. They had no idea what impact some of the family dynamics would have on my life choices. And they never physically abused me nor did I ever see or know of any time when my father physically abused my mother. Most women who become battered wives were raised in a dysfunctional home. We respond to it by shutting off our feelings and dancing as fast as we can to try to make everyone happy so, in turn, we will get love. Unfortunately, we do not have the power to make "them" show us love. We are dancing for nothing.

CINDERELLA

In my teen years, I had two experiences, which had a tremendous impact on my future life choices. The first began when I was fifteen. I met Jake. How can I describe the magical encounter we had? While we talked for hours, a well of love sprung up within each of us as if we had always been together and always would be. We had the rare experience of somehow "knowing" the goodness within the other's spirit. Suddenly I was totally accepted and approved of by someone who mattered more to me than anyone else in the world. We were two emotionally needy teenagers just dying for love and here it was. From that point on and for the next five years, our love only grew. I no longer felt rejected or internally alone. We were fortunate to experience genuine emotional intimacy.

Then we rode off on a white horse while the birds sang and the sun shone. Oh no; that's the other story I wanted to be in, Cinderella. I have wondered in my life after Jake, if experiencing that kind of love was a blessing or a curse. Truly it was a blessing for many reasons. My shattered sense of self was temporarily solidified and I felt pure happiness. The curse is that once you have experienced love so grand, how can you settle for less?

Jake and I spent the next five years of our lives loving each other, laughing a lot and getting into drugs. Oops, not a good thing to do. What did we know? We both came from families that drank freely so what was the difference if we included some substances? Neither of us had parents who kept any kind of reins on us. We were free to do whatever we wanted, whenever we wanted, and we did. This is NOT a good setup for teenagers. Teenagers need very clear parental boundaries on their behavioral choices. What happened to us proved this to be true.

THE PAINFUL CHOICE

When I was 18 we shared an experience that even after 30 years causes a sharp pain deep within my soul. I am not over it and never will be. It is not something I can fully work through. Rarely have I discussed it with anyone although it is always in the back of my mind. I have had many women in therapy recount their similar experiences to me with the same intensity of anguish I feel. I proceed here with reluctance and remorse, yet this issue needs to be addressed because I believe it was a factor in my future unhealthy choice for a marital partner.

Throughout my childhood I yearned for the day when I would be a mother. Being very maternal, I would dress up my pet cat in doll clothes and put her in a buggy, making her stay there while I walked my "baby." I loved dolls, my favorite being a rubber baby doll that drank from a bottle then peed all over. She had a ripped, broken nose but I loved her. Symbolic or what? Jake and I would often talk about what it would be like when we got married and had children. We would discuss their names and which features of both of us we would want them to have.

Jake and I were having many problems after I graduated from high school, primarily because of his erratic behavior from his substance abuse and my codependent need to take care of him and try to "make" him act responsibly. Then in September just when I was starting college I thought I might be pregnant. I was very frightened and had no one to turn to. I had heard that if a woman took a massive dose of "quinine" pills, than her period would begin. Desperate, I tried it and ended up overdosing on the pills. I got very sick but my cycle did not begin. I didn't know what to do. I wanted to mother this baby.

I could not go to Jake, who was my closest friend, because he was in some teenage drug-induced state. And I was too afraid of my mother's reaction to confide in her. Remember I had devoted my life to trying to make my mother happy and I knew this would enrage her. After all, what would the neighbors think?

I considered suicide just to escape, but called the suicide hotline before doing anything to harm myself. They referred me to an OB/GYN near my home. I remember going there in my mini-skirt with knee socks on my skinny body and with my long hair pulled back in a ponytail with a bow. Although I was 18, I probably looked more like a pathetic 12 years old. The doctor was a warm, compassionate man who would remain a part of my life for many years. As a matter of fact, he was the attending doctor when I gave birth to my son a few years later. Although he was obviously very busy he talked with me for about two hours while I cried hysterically once he confirmed my suspicions. I wanted to marry Jake and have our baby. I did not know what to do. I could not face the wrath of my mother and the complicated drug issues that Jake was dealing with. I was so confused and so very alone. I needed a parent desperately for guidance and clarity.

The doctor became the voice of compassion I was longing for. He strongly suggested I go to New York to see a colleague of his to have an abortion. They were not legal at that time in our state. Although I did not believe in abortion, I felt like I had no other choice. It seemed to be the only answer. I had no one I could turn to for help with raising a child and I was just a kid myself. Ironically or maybe not, I ended up raising two children alone just a few years later anyway. So here was this educated, kind father figure telling me that going to New York was the right answer to my problem. He made all of the arrangements while I sat there crying.

I went to Jake's house when I left the doctor's office and told him everything. I knew how much he loved me, but I also knew that he was too weak at that point in his life to be of any help to me. In the years since, we have often shared our remorse over this decision. We were two lost souls; too weak to stand up and take charge of what we both knew instinctively would have been the right decision for us. The abortion was not the right answer, but it appeared to be the only one.

For many months afterwards I withdrew into myself while I grieved intensely. This reinforced my already existing feelings of shame deep inside of me. I developed a paranoid fear that I would be punished for what I had done. In retrospect I have often wondered what role that fear played in my future choice to marry an abusive man. So many women I have seen in therapy end up punishing themselves subconsciously in some way after having an abortion. Society, as a whole, does not understand the emotional cost of that act. There is a natural bonding process beginning at the time of conception deep within the woman's soul. If a pregnancy ends prematurely, the bonding causes intense grieve with the loss. Unfortunately, this aspect of abortion is rarely discussed. As much as I loved Jake, our love could not survive after this painful experience. Too much emotional damage had been done. But I'm getting a head of my story.

THE PEACEFUL CHOICE

Shortly after that painful episode was the second experience, which would prove to be the most important of my life. It began when my sister, Marcia, moved to California about the time that I was graduating from high school. She ended up living in a big house in the Hollywood Hills with some friends next door to a Christian singing group. At first she thought her neighbors were pretty weird. She would call and tell me about these happy people that were always singing and praying. After awhile she not only got involved in the Jesus movement of the '70s, she got engaged to a musician from the house next door.

I was not sure what to expect when Jake and I flew to California for Marcia and Eddie's wedding. My mother had raised us in the Catholic Church, which did not promote much of a personal relationship with God at that time. When I was younger I knew I loved God with my whole little heart, but as I got into my teens I shelved those feelings.

Upon arrival, Marcia took me to meet Annie who was part of the singing group. Annie greeted us with hugs and warmth. Something I hungered for. She sat at the piano and began to sing for me with the most beautiful voice I had ever heard. Her eyes were closed and she appeared to be communing with God. The room was suddenly filled with overwhelming peace and love. It was a holy experience. I knew that I was in the presence of God and suddenly I felt loved, healed and forgiven. I did not understand what was happening but I knew that it was good and it was real. It is an experience that I have come to depend on in life to keep everything in balance and harmony. Practicing the presence of God is a very cool way to live. At times it is the only way to survive.

My love of God from childhood was renewed. The way I perceived life, changed. I was suddenly able to transcend my view of reality to see things from a higher spiritual plane. Little did I know that my relationship with God was to keep me sane through the insanity of the years to come. After I came home I discovered that the '70s were a great time to become a Christian. Bible studies were held in homes, coffeehouses, underground meeting rooms and schools. It was exciting and so alive and fit well with this "hippie" era.

Jake was with me in California but claimed that he was an atheist and he could not share in my newfound passion. The gap widened. My love for Jake never lessened, but I could not understand what his problem was. It was so clear to me that this was the greatest thing we had ever encountered. Better than any drug. I could not understand why he was being so resistant. How could he deny the existence of God? It was so simple, all he had to do was open his eyes and look around to see the daily miracles of life. I did not realize back then that every person has his or her own individual spiritual journey. This was the first time we were in such opposition.

Then there was the sex. I now believed sex was to be reserved for marriage. Considering that we had years of fabulous, uninhibited sex, Jake probably did not know where in the world I was coming from. This was a tough one because we were incredibly drawn to each other sexually. I mean to tell you that Jake was one hot hunk, he looked like a young Marlon Brando and he was definitely cool. I had no other experience to compare it to, but I was quite sure that it was the best of the best.

Although I was only nineteen I thought I needed to be married because I did not think I could maintain the celibacy gig for long. So I was suddenly sober and celibate and Jake was in the same space we had been. It is clear I was a confused, young girl. Saved, but confused. And thus, my story of abuse begins.

The Marriage

Chapter Three: The Elephant of Abuse

November 25, 1972
To My Honey,
Love was just an image, which I could take no hold
It came upon me as a shadow
hovering over all that I had known
The immense undertow of that emotion
holds strongly to my heart
Now it is impossible to fly so freely
as I once so easily had
For you, Tommy, are within me
from which I could never part.
Love,
Me
(The poem I wrote Tommy on our wedding day. Little did I
know how true it was.)

I met Tommy in Fort Lauderdale during the Easter break of
my second year of college. Fort Lauderdale was a wild time
and there was no way I could maintain my sobriety. In my
deluded state Tommy appeared to be the answer to my prayers.
When we returned home we began dating and he immediately

wanted to make plans to get married. He was quite handsome and had a wonderful, funny personality. He focused all his attention on me and made me feel like a precious jewel to be treated with tenderness.

I was thrilled when he confessed to being a practicing Christian and began going to Bible studies with me. Tommy was almost impossible to resist; he was like a dream come true. I assumed I could have the emotional closeness with him I had with Jake. That was one of my greatest errors in judgment.

Within a few months I started to see disturbing personality traits in Tommy that I began to wonder about. One time he overreacted when Jake stopped by to return an old album of mine. I was kind of flattered it bothered Tommy so much that he yelled for a while and threw the album across the room. The intensity of his reaction did make me very uncomfortable, but I wrote it off as jealousy. Another time he and his brother got into a fight, which evolved into pushing and hitting while screaming profanities. Never having brothers, I didn't know if this behavior was normal or not. I knew that it frightened me. As time went on, Tommy began to be critical of my family and friends. I felt like he disapproved of me if I spent time with them. Actually, I was beginning to feel like he disapproved of many things about me. I had experienced rejection all of my life from my father and knew I did not want to go through that again with the man I chose to marry.

After awhile I began to miss the closeness and unconditional acceptance I had with Jake. But about that time, guess what? I was pregnant again. Ms. Fertile Myrtle. Oh boy. I went to Jake first and told him. We cried together, and then he asked me to marry him. We both knew abortion was out of the question. Jake said he would raise my child as his own. That is what I really wanted to do but I thought the "right" thing to do was marrying Tommy and devote myself to him.

I was one young girl in desperate need of guidance. Once

again, I had no adult to turn to for advice. Parents, please keep the lines of communication open with your teens. Pregnancy is not a good reason to marry. But I resigned myself to the fact that I would marry Tommy and make this a good marriage. I did love Tommy, but I could not get close to him like I was with Jake. He seemed to have a defensive wall around him.

I thought that once I decided to marry Tommy it would not be right to have any communication with Jake. It broke my heart, but I broke off my relationship with Jake and went forward with my new life with Tommy and our baby. We would be a family and I was very excited about having our baby.

Two weeks prior to our wedding, Tommy's sister asked me if I knew about his "temper." I wasn't sure what she was talking about. Was she referring to his behavior that made me so uncomfortable? When I questioned her further she clammed up. I had only known Tommy about six months at this point. What did I really know about him?

THE MARRIAGE

My first exposure to his temper was on our honeymoon. We were in the Bahamas and Tommy got mad because I wanted to buy a gift for my mother. Mad is an understatement. Tommy went into a rage. His face was transformed into an evil looking contortion and he repeatedly called me a "fucking bitch." No one had ever spoken to me like that before. I could not believe that the man I had just married, whose child I was carrying, was speaking to me in such a cruel way. I was devastated. I sat huddled in a corner on the floor, crying. This continued for about an hour while he threw things around the room. I was immobilized with fear.

Finally, I ran out and sat on the beach wondering what in the world I had gotten myself into. I was five months pregnant, twenty years old and married to a lunatic. But I made a vow to myself that night to be a perfect, loving wife to Tommy. I would dance as fast as I could for him in an attempt to heal his internal wounds. I thought my love and prayers would heal his rage. Little did I know I had not seen anything yet.

When I returned to the room he was over it and was laughing and joking, ready to go out for the evening. I was still heartbroken and frightened. He said I should not have made him mad. Somehow it had become my fault. But that was his pattern. When it was over in his mind, I was expected to forget about the episode. That night when we had sex, part of me died inside. How could I make love to a man who had just treated me that way? In the years to come I would often wish that I could somehow remove my head and just let him use my body for sex. This was not the mutual lovemaking I knew with Jake.

When living with an abuser, survival often means shutting down more and more of yourself inside (i.e. "removing my head"). Slowly you die to self because self is your soul. It is the healthy, vibrant, authentic person in you that God created. Accepting abuse is not in the picture of caring for the soul; it destroys it.

During the marriage I went for counseling with our pastor. He told me to harden myself and put up with the abuse because divorce was not scriptural. Now I cringe when I think of those words. He was so wrong. God would never want me to harden myself nor to accept abuse.

With Tommy I came to realize towards the end that it did not matter if I was an absolute angel or a total witch, his abusive episodes were triggered internally and had nothing to do with what I said or did. I remember another well meaning Christian telling me if I kept praying for Tommy, the rage would come out of his mouth like a puff of smoke. Well, I prayed my heart out for him daily and so did my friends, yet I never saw that puff of smoke. One thing that we cannot change through prayer is another person's will.

THE PHYSICAL ABUSE BEGINS

But I was thrilled about the upcoming birth. I could not wait to hold my baby in my arms. Tommy got involved in Lamaze classes with me and although he continued to have rage episodes, my hopes were up that things would now be normal. My girlfriends threw me a baby shower and I was so excited about every precious little baby item for my baby. "My baby"; how wonderful that sounded to me.

When I came home from the shower I put all of the gifts out in the living room for Tommy to share with me. I had a plate of delicious food from the baby shower waiting for him when he got home. He walked in with an angry look on his face and became enraged because I had not "cooked" for him. He then proceeded to call me every filthy name in the book while kicking the presents repeatedly around the room. If I had a dollar for every time he called me a "fucking bitch," I would be a wealthy woman today.

This went on for at least an hour. I was sitting on the couch, sobbing. He picked up the plate of food and threw it against the wall about two inches above my head. I was so scared. Food went flying everywhere and fell onto my hair and clothes. The grease marks stayed on the wall until we moved out months later. I stood up to try to leave the room; he grabbed me by the arm and threw me back onto the couch. He continued to scream at me about two inches from my face while he held my throat. I was choking, but he continued. I could feel the heat from his breath while his spit covered my face.

His eyes had the crazed look of an animal about to kill the enemy. All I could think of was that his face looked so evil and he was going to kill either the baby or me. The memory is still so vivid it gives me the creeps to think about it. There was no reasoning left with this creature. My heart was pounding so hard, I felt like I was going to collapse. He ended by covering my face with his huge fist and threatening to kill me by crushing my face. This gesture with his fist to my face was to become a common practice.

Within an hour he was fine and wanted to talk about the shower. By then I was having severe Braxton Hicks contractions (false labor) but I did not dare tell him because he might get angry. He wanted me to apologize to him for getting him upset although I had no idea what his reasoning was. I was too frightened to oppose him, fearing he would go into another rage. I had difficulty not crying and tried to pretend that everything was fine. I picked up the gifts that had been kicked around the room. That night tears streamed down my face during the act of sex. He never noticed.

The next day when my arms, throat and face were covered with bruises Tommy told me to stay home. I called his mother for help. She said to just keep my mouth shut with Tommy because a person "can't argue alone." The abuse had nothing to do with arguing. I called my mother and it was clear she did not want to hear about it. This denial is a common reaction by family members when abuse occurs. It's not right, but it's the way it is. For God's sake, I was nine months pregnant. Three weeks later I gave birth. Even more than twenty years later, I am crying as I recall these events. I can still remember the intense sorrow and fear I felt over Tommy's behavior and by the lack of support from those around me.

But we had a wonderful natural birth experience with our daughter. The labor and delivery was only four hours long and was textbook perfect. Tommy was an excellent coach and he seemed as thrilled as I was with the birth of our precious Danialle. Without bias, she was the most beautiful baby ever born. It was quite an event with most of our extended family waiting at the hospital. We had a large group of friends and everyone seemed to get into the excitement of her birth. It was a very special time and I thought now that we had Danialle things would be different. Wrong again.

The abuse increased in frequency and intensity. I cannot remember how many times I would be holding Danialle and nursing her when he would be yelling at me with my face squeezed in his hand. The pain of my teeth cutting into my cheeks was almost unbearable but I tried to stay calm and breathe slowly for the sake of my baby. It was a time when Tommy knew I was immobilized so he had me. Was it any wonder that Dani was colicky, which just further enraged him?

When Danialle would cry, I was told over and over again to make her "shut the fuck up." Every night he wanted a meal on the table with me eating with him without the baby crying. If she did, the food went flying. Dani was so precious and innocent; I did not understand how he could act so ugly around our baby.

Intermixed with these times were the fun times with friends and family, which always gave me hope. You see, when Tommy was good, he was very, very good. He just had a charming way about him that was so appealing. Who would believe that this charismatic man could be so mean? In fact, most people did not. I understood because I also wanted to deny there was any abuse. I was ashamed that I was being treated this way. And Tommy could be my friend at times. But when Tommy was bad, he was very, very bad.

One night Tommy chased me around the house with a knife threatening to kill me. I was so scared. I locked myself in the bathroom with Danialle and yelled as loud as I could. We lived in a townhouse and I was hoping that someone would hear me. I felt like I was screaming to save my life; I probably was. The man next door came over to see what was wrong. Tommy told him I was having postpartum problems, so he left. Once again, it became my fault. I went and stayed at my mother's home for a few days after that but I knew she did not want me there.

I went back to Tommy. He swore it would be different from now on. I called the police to find out what kind of protection they could give me, but none was available back then. I felt so alone in this hellish existence. My sweet next-door neighbor brought me over some candy a couple of days later thinking that I was having a depression problem. I probably should have told him the truth, but I was not yet ready to come out of denial.

Jake called me one day a few weeks after the knife incident. I was terrified that Tommy would find out, although he was at work. Jake had heard about what was going on from a close friend of mine and he begged me to leave Tommy before he killed me. I told him I couldn't do that because Tommy was my husband and I did not believe in divorce, it was not Biblical. As if abuse is Biblical. Then I asked him to never call me again. I hung up and cried for days because I missed my relationship with Jake so much. It seemed like a lifetime ago. Because reality was too difficult to handle emotionally, I spent my days reminiscing about those years in high school when I was popular and treated so nicely by my friends. I wanted to share my children and my life with someone who would treat us with respect, like Jake. I missed him so much but I believed I had to deny myself contact with him to make it work with Tommy.

UNREALISTIC HOPE

I decided it was time to get pregnant again because I thought, for some odd reason, that if we had two children, Tommy would settle down. Within a couple of months I was pregnant and very happy about it. Abused women tend to delude themselves by creating a reason for why it will now be different. I guess it is a way of creating hope and avoiding reality. Tommy was happy about the pregnancy and for a time, things were relatively calm. One day when I was about six months pregnant Tommy came home enraged. Of course, there was no apparent reason. Once again the food I had waiting on the table for his arrival went flying, then he turned on me.

As my two year old daughter watched, he threw me up against the wall, pulled me off the floor and onto the couch. He continued his ongoing theme of what a "fucking bitch" I was. As I begged him not to hurt the baby, he mocked me with a very ugly, evil, distorted face and sarcastic tone to his voice. At one point he lifted his arm with his fist clenched, threatening to punch my extended belly. I was unable to move because he had a firm grip on my throat. It hurt so much. I began praying out loud that my baby would not be hurt. Tommy pulled my hair and pinched my face while screaming at me to "shut the fuck up." I quit voicing my prayers, but they continued in my head; they were my mental salvation. My arms felt like they were being crushed as he held them and shook me violently. My head was being tossed like a rag doll. I could not stop crying. When I looked into his eyes I thought I was looking at the face of the devil. Danialle stood there watching, wide-eyed and crying. He told her I made him act this way, that it was my fault.

When he was done he went into another room to watch TV while I lay there sobbing and trying to comfort my little girl. My entire body was in pain, but not as much as my broken heart. I could not understand how one person could treat another with such cruelty. Then he left to go to the bar. I tried calling my sister to come get me but the only person I could get a hold of was his sister. She came and got Danialle and me and took us to her house. There was no way to deny the abuse when she saw my swollen lip and the bruises. And, besides, she was the one who had originally warned me about his temper. She let us spend the night and was very kind to us until she spoke to her parents. Then she told me we would have to leave. She treated me like I had done something wrong. Sure, I was telling the truth about an ugly family secret.

Danialle and I went back to my mother's house and she was

not thrilled about us being at her home. The next day I went to my doctor to make sure the baby was okay. I was bruised all over by then. He said, "Go home immediately and pack clothes for you and Danialle. You must leave Tommy because he is going to kill you. Do you hear me? He is going to kill you." I had nowhere to go.

By this time Jake was dating a close friend of mine so he heard about this episode of violence. He called me at my mother's home and told me he would pay for Danialle and me to take the train to California to stay with Marcia and Eddie. My mom came with us. I was six months pregnant and had my two year old on my lap on a train for three days, but at least I knew we were safe. Fortunately, Danialle was a wonderful, easygoing child. Marcia and Eddie told me I could stay and live with them until I had the baby. They loved Danialle, which thrilled me. I, once again, did not know what to do. I did not feel like I should interfere with their lives, remember I was used to "dancing" for everyone. They didn't have any children and a household is very different once children are living there. And I had no money. What would I do once the baby was born?

Tommy began calling and begging me to come home. He swore that this time it would definitely be different. He would never touch me again. He wanted to share the birth of the new baby with me. And I knew we did have such a wonderful birth experience with Danialle. I went back, wanting to believe him and keep the family intact. Foolishly, I went back. Of course, the rage continued.

INCREASING INTENSITY AND FREQUENCY

Tommy and I shared a wonderful birth experience when our son, Josh, was born. He weighed almost 11 pounds so it was a difficult natural delivery. Tommy had to get up on the table and help push the baby out. Well, we did it and Josh was the most lovable baby ever born. But because Joshua was so big and I was so thin, I was pretty ripped up inside. My doctor apologized to me for not doing a C-section and ordered me to bed for a month. I knew this was totally unrealistic, given my situation. If Tommy did not have me catering to him, I knew he would become enraged.

For the first two weeks after the birth, Marcia came from California to help and my mother and Janis came over daily. They were very respectful of Tommy and were a Godsend to me. When Marcia left, Tommy once again became the bully and ordered my mother and Janis out of the house. He told them not to come back. Uh-oh, I knew what was coming. How I wished, in those days, I had a supportive father or a really, really big brother. Or a mother with a strong, supportive personality.

A couple of days later Janis came over to help me while Tommy was working. He came home early and told her to get out. Tommy began to scream out of control about the nerve of my "fucking" sister for parking in our driveway. What did this have to do with anything? For heaven's sake, we lived on a main road. I felt panic go through my entire body. My sore, weary body became braced for a battle. He proceeded to pull me out of the bed and throw me across the room and onto the floor.

As Tommy screamed profanities at me, his vile spit covered Josh's little face as I was breast-feeding him. Tommy held my cheeks so tight that my teeth began to ache as they cut the inside of my mouth. Blood started to drip out of my mouth and onto my baby while he tried to suckle. This continued for about an hour. And after the long period of being shoved, grabbed, shaken and pinched; I fainted. I came to with Tommy kicking me all over my body, including my stomach. He was yelling that I was faking. What kind of person does this to another? He continued his ongoing theme of what a "fucking bitch" I was. My God, I had just given birth to his son. I felt like I was a prisoner being tortured at the hands of a madman. My stomach was cramping up in terrible pain. My crying turning into quiet moans as he held my throat and screamed in my face. He held me so tightly; I could hardly swallow. His breath had a bitter stench that I thought must be coming from the rage inside him. His face had an evil, sickening look to it. His eyes were void of any feeling. They were empty.

Danialle stood there crying for her mommy. She kept telling her daddy to stop hurting mommy. Once again, he said that I made him do it. When he went to the bathroom I snuck to the phone and called my sister. I told her to call the police because this was the time he was going to kill me. She made the mistake of calling Tommy's father for help. He came over and promptly told Tommy that my mother made him come over but he did not believe this was any of his business. As if my timid, insecure mother could stand up to any man and make him do something. Like most abusive men, Tommy denied the abuse and would probably swear even today with his life that no abuse occurred; and believe it. Tommy has managed to keep himself in a protective bubble of denial with his family. It is the big, pink elephant in their living room that no one acknowledges.

With disdain his father asked me if I wanted a ride anywhere. As if I would get in the car with my precious babies with this incredibly cold man. I had enough abuse from that family for one day. I realize now that his father was not capable of caring about me because emotionally he did not want to face the pink elephant of abuse. Tommy's parents resented me for bringing the ugly elephant out in the open. I would not go along with their game of distorting reality. I could not or I would probably have ended up dead. So his father left. Tommy left and went to the bar. He thought everything was fine because, after all, it was over as far as he was concerned. My sister came over to get us and, once again,

I went to my mother's house but this time with two babies.

Later that same night I ended up at the emergency room due to severe abdominal pain because I was bleeding internally. Like most abused women I lied and said I had fallen down the stairs. When I called the police the next day for protection, I was told to come to the station to have pictures taken of the bruises. Right! I had just given birth, been beaten up by my husband and I was going to go strip for the male police. I don't think so.

I stayed at my mother's home over the holidays and was too embarrassed to tell relatives why I was there. They may have known but no one talked about it. In retrospect, it would have been nice to have someone reach out to me with compassion, but when it comes to domestic violence no one wants to get involved. Just recently I learned there is a long history of wife abuse in my lineage and it was always handled with denial. Now I understand why no one was reaching out to help me if they suspected there was abuse. It was the same song and dance. Within a month I was back with Tommy wanting to believe the same promises. The abusive episodes continued.

THE FINAL BLOW

The event that became the last straw occurred a few months later. After closing the bars one night Tommy came home in a rage. What a surprise. The children and I were asleep in our beds. He woke me up by screaming obscenities, grabbed my arm and pulled me out of the bed. He threw me across the room into the hall where I hit the wall and fell to the floor. I knew by the evil look in his face that this could be the time he would finally kill me. He had that empty look in his eyes. He was clearly way out of control and had been drinking. Substance abuse was not always a part of the abusive episodes, but it was this night and I feared for my life. Most of the men in my extended family had been alcoholics and it was not a pretty picture. I had seen enough bizarre behavior while I was growing up to know what impact alcohol could have on a person. Tommy was out of control enough without any drugs, so I could only imagine what he was capable of when he was under the influence.

I scrambled to my feet and ran into the children's room. What I saw when I opened their door still breaks my heart to think about. It made me realize I had to escape for my children's sanity. Innocent little Danialle was sitting up in her bed, sucking her thumb, holding her covers around herself and crying. Although only a few months old, Josh had pulled himself up and was standing in his crib listening to Tommy's rage with such a frightened expression on his precious face. Oh God, how could these little babies that I love so much be exposed to such insanity? I had to get them away from him. I needed to plan an escape. I could no longer stay hidden behind the cloak of denial. His insanity was now impacting my babies who I loved more than life itself. The charade was over, I was going to find a way to get my precious children out of this craziness. Maybe I was not capable of doing it for me but, by the grace of God, I would do it for them.

LIGHT IN THE DARKNESS

The next day I called my doctor, my friend, for the name and number of a therapist. I went to see Pat, the therapist he recommended, the next day. I am quite certain that God used her to help save my children and me. She cried as I told her about my situation. She told me she was very frightened for me because I could tell my story without a hint of emotion. I realize now that being so shut down emotionally can be an indicator of someone who is suicidal. Which I was, except that I would not leave my children. She told me that no one, not even a dog, should be treated like I was. She said I was A WORTHY WOMAN who should not accept abuse as my lot in life. Respect and kindness should be a given in any relationship. There is NO excuse for abuse. I knew somewhere within me that it was true.

Pat called me that night at home because she was so worried about me. Her kindness still brings tears to my eyes. She became the healthy parental figure I so desperately needed. Within a few sessions I began to believe it was possible for me to get out with my kids and start a new life. Tommy liked the fact that I was in therapy because it confirmed that I was the "crazy" one. It is what he had been saying all along. I agreed with him so I could continue going. I knew that I could not stay sane living in this insane situation with him. It is almost impossible to stay sane in the midst of insanity.

Finding a place for my children and me to live proved to be a major problem. No one wanted to rent to a single mother living on welfare. I knew I would have to be on welfare initially just to survive. The thought of welfare terrified me, but not as much as the thought of what the abuse would do to my children. I would just have to buck up and endure it. Pride had to take a back seat to survival. I had no money and no one was going to give me any. Some people have families to support them; I was not that fortunate. I knew there was no way that Tommy was going to pay child support no matter what the courts may tell him. No way. So as much as I kicked and screamed about going on welfare, I had no choice.

My mother owned a two-family home; she lived in the lower flat. It was the home that I had grown up in. Throughout my childhood she had let strangers, family members and friends rent the small upper flat. My older sister had lived there with her son when she had gone through a divorce. It was totally separate from the lower flat where my mother and stepfather lived. I did not really want to go back to that neighborhood as a divorced mother, but it looked like it was my only option. "What will the neighbors think?" was drilled into my head, so I was humiliated by my situation even though it was all about survival. But the worst part was when I asked my mother if I could rent the flat, she refused to let me and my babies move in. Can you imagine how that made me feel? I mean I was talking about life and death survival for us. Sometimes it is very difficult to understand why people choose to make certain decisions.

One evening a couple of weeks after I asked my mother about the flat, she was baby-sitting for the kids while Tommy and I went bowling on our league (not my choice for a good time). When we got home, Tommy went into one of his "fuck this and fuck that" verbal rages in front of my mother. When he went downstairs she said, "That's what you live with?" Hello, where have you been for the last four years? Had she not heard what I had been telling her, had she not seen the bruises? Why did she think I had escaped to her home on a regular basis with babies in tow? It was certainly not because I wanted to go stay somewhere with my children where I was not wanted. My mother is not typically a cold, heartless person like this sounds, but in this situation the uncompassionate curse of denial was definitely at play.

For the first time in my life I stood up to my mother and told her that if she did not let me and my babies move into her upper flat, she would never see us again. This was very hard for me to do because I had spent my life trying to get her approval. But when it came to our survival, I had to step outside my insecurities and take a stand. She said I could rent the flat. When she told the current tenants they had to move she found out the woman's sister had been murdered by her husband! Family members had not taken her seriously either and now she was dead. I think it was a wake up call for my mother.

So now I had a place to move, but where in the world was I going to get the money to move? Pat found an anonymous donor who just out and out gave me the money. I have no idea who that person was or why they were willing to help me out. It amazed me that someone wanted to help a woman who was being abused by her spouse. It had been my experience thus far that no one really cared. God bless that person. I found it so sad that a stranger would reach out to help me when those closest to me just turned their backs and chose to ignore "the elephant." But now, I was getting out. During that time, I kept a journal that I will now share with you.

Chapter Four: My Journal

October 26, 1976

Hey, I'm surviving, day-by-day, hour-by-hour, and minute-by-minute. I'm not feeling much guilt today. Mostly impatience. How much longer am I going to have to endure the pretense of a marriage? Marriage! What a joke. How many other women have suffered the humiliation of wife abuse, mental and physical? Oh dear Lord, if I survive the days ahead let me help others from ever experiencing such a horrible existence. Or should I say nonexistence. With each episode of abuse I was becoming more and more of a non-person, only to be taken out when necessary. Why, why was I so blind? Why didn't I get out sooner? Four years of leaving and coming back. Four years of living on hopes, refusing to give up on my childhood dream of a lifelong, wonderful marriage. Each incident makes me cringe. The constant everyday humiliation and degrading is too hard.

My therapist is right. I am boiling over with rage. And hurt. I'm ready to burst. Oh Lord, let me hang on. How much longer must I endure this suffering before the people move out from my mother's flat so we can move in? I am so scared. Will we make it? I have no choice. Staying here would cause me to burst and go insane just to escape this horrid, horrid life and all its horrid memories. How could a man beat and torture his "wife" right after childbirth? While their two and a half year old watches and cries. For hours yet. He is so sick!

He's furious today because I enrolled Danialle in ballet. How dare I spend $7.00! Does that mean he will go berserk tonight? It is a thin line between a beating and a murder. Oh Lord, get me out of here. My life for the last four years has been a living hell. Why did I marry such a sick bastard? I certainly had my choice. Why? Through therapy I will find out why and never make such an error again. From ages twenty through twenty-four I have been dreaming of the past, when I used to be happy. Living in the past at age twenty. How horribly sad! I felt I had no way out and I didn't. It had to come to this extreme of me almost losing my mind before I could face reality. For so long I locked all of these horrid things in my subconscious only to come out periodically. But now I see it all so clearly and I am freaked out.

How could one human being treat another so cruel? His wife yet. Oh God, I am filled with such hate and rage. Help me. How has it all affected Danialle? Will she grow up believing that it's alright to abuse others or worse yet, to be abused? She is everything to me. I cannot handle the thought of my perfect, bright little girl ever suffering because of sick Tommy. Please Lord; quicken to her heart only the good. Please. Oh Jesus, you love her more than I do. A love I cannot even comprehend. Do not let any harm come to my precious daughter. Please let me be getting out in time, please. Thank God that Joshua is only eleven months old. I am sure that he is too young to be influenced to any great extent.

I am going to end for today. I'm getting too upset. I'll go have a bowl of ice cream and escape for a couple minutes.

October 28, 1976

Well, I am still here waiting and watching. When will the next blow up be? I've come to another reality. There is not one thing I do right according to Tommy. Can you imagine an existence of constant degrading? That is mine. Funny, because from other people I always hear how spotless my house is, how good I cook, how thrifty I am, what a good mother I am, how strong I must be to manage a home, the kids and a job, how I always look and dress good. But have I ever heard this from Tommy or been appreciated for all I do? Oh no, heaven forbid. Thank God for other people filling my ego, otherwise I would probably have committed suicide by now. I have come close. I even left the final note to my beautiful children. Tommy came home, saw the note and laughed. He dared me to take the pills then shoved them in my mouth and held my mouth shut very tightly for a longtime. Fortunately, I did not swallow them. When I would cry all day for days he would tell me to "shut the fuck up and quit being so miserable." That really helped. These were the times when I would face the reality of my horrid life just briefly and be overwhelmed. Thank God I see it all now.

When I had mastitis with a temp of 106 degrees due to a plugged milk duct in my breast from nursing Josh, Tommy told me I was "a fucking bitch" and to "shut up and go to bed." All night I was shaking horribly from a chill and in the morning he refused to get up and make the children breakfast. I had to while I was in the middle of throwing up! He was so mad that he had to take the time out to take me to the doctor. That bastard, how could he treat another human, especially his wife, so cruel? How horribly sick. Why? Why? Why me?

Last night I could not sleep thinking about the move. I am such a nervous wreck. My therapist said from the outside you would never know that a thing was wrong with me. Inside I am a total wreck.

I am actually afraid that Tommy will find a way to murder me once I move out. It is a thin line between a beating and a killing. When a person goes crazy, they go crazy. I do not feel like I have any strength left to make it. Please God, pull me along. I have to force myself to keep my mind together. Thank God for Pat. She has helped me so much. I know that the Lord brought her to me. She understands everything so clearly and helps me to put things in their right perspective. She has helped me to see an unbiased reality. She has saved my life. And I mean that with everything within me. Because I know where my mind was at after being treated so inhumanely for four years.

Peter, a friend who grew up with Tommy, has told me many times that to him "I am the shining example of what every man wants." He also says that I am "A WORTHY WOMAN." I hang on to his words to help get me through. I think that it is true somewhere in my mind but I have been so degraded and humiliated I cannot really believe it. Isn't it funny that Peter, being in prison, would be the person to help me so much? I have always sensed his beautiful spirit no matter what crime he has committed. Why is it in our society that a man selling drugs is punished, which he should be, but a man who beats his wife is allowed to be free? Somehow, someday I am going to work to change that.

Today Danialle is going to be a tiger at her nursery school Halloween party. Thank you Lord, for my children, they are such a blessing! Danialle and Joshua both give me so much love. Please Lord do not let me take any of this out on them. Please help me!!

NOTE: Peter Wrightman died about a year later. I hope that he is eternally blessed for his kindness shown towards me when I so desperately needed it.

October 31, 1976

Thank God for Pat. If only everyone could find someone who could help them so perfectly. We are going to find out what in my subconscious caused me to choose someone like Tommy. It seems as though I have a deep-rooted shame inside stemming from childhood, which makes me feel unworthy, and like I deserved to be punished and hurt. That is why I have never been able to say "no" to people, whether the end result would hurt me or not. I don't know how to care about my feelings. But I will learn.

November 1, 1976

How strange life is. Yesterday we had a really nice day. Tommy took us out to dinner with him then to his mom's house so Danialle could go trick or treating with her cousin. His parents were being really nice. They bought Joshua a toy that he just loves. It was a perfect day. So naturally I start getting my hopes up again. But there is something I have realized; I am a worthy woman. I deserve to be treated with kindness every day. Being treated nice once a month or so is not enough. I have to realize that the kids and I deserve to be treated nice and as people with feelings on a day-to-day basis. It is very hard for me to feel worthy. It is funny because I never realized this in me before but now that I look back I see it was always there. I felt I had to keep on top of things and be in control because I was not worthy of having anyone take care of me. How many other abused women feel this way?

The big dilemma now is that the couple will be out of mom's flat by Saturday, November 13th. I have to move on Monday or Tuesday because I need Janis to help me. Well Monday, the 15th, is Joshua's first birthday! Tuesday the 16th I have an appointment for my job as a skin care consultant, plus the kids have a doctor's appointment. So should I have a family birthday party for Josh on Sunday then move on

Monday? Could I handle that emotionally? I can't wait until
the following week because that is Thanksgiving week, which
is another story. What do I do? I am going to discuss it with
Pat. I have two weeks to get things ready. I am so scared!!!!!

November 3, 1976

I am getting excited and anxious now. There is so much to
do. The flat is darling. Mom wants the first month's rent,
where am I going to get it? ADC (welfare) takes six weeks to
begin. Doesn't she understand that I have to buy basics like
food plus a million other things? The real clincher is that mom
has made it clear that she could be getting more for the rent
than what she is charging me although it's more than what the
last people were paying. Talk about making me feel unworthy!
Life is so hard to understand. Lord, help me from ever treating
another person like that. I have always believed that mom was
so perfect. I was not facing reality just like I distorted it with
Tommy. Will I ever find someone to love me in all of reality?
Gosh, I hope if Danialle or Josh ever need me, I will be there
loving them.
NOTE: In retrospect, I realize that my mother has always loved
me but was not free to show it because of her insecurities
stemming from her childhood. I have to give my mother credit
because she did do a much better job of parenting then her
parents. Hopefully, each generation will continue to take a
giant step towards good mental and spiritual health.

November 8, 1976

Today I went to ADC. What a drag! Looking around at the
people I wonder if they have ever heard of soap or shampoo. I
mean, really, someone vomited in the chair next to me while I
was waiting. Today has been very hard. I am scared. Mom, Ed
(stepfather) and Janis started painting the flat today. I worked
on cleaning the kitchen. It is good to know that everything will

be nice and clean when we move in. I am so frightened. I just want to escape. Pat has so much faith in me. She wants me to get right back in school and get my degree. She says that it would be the best thing for me, to be doing something constructive. The state would pay for nursery school. Danialle would love it. But Joshie is so young!! What to do? I feel like I am ready to burst. I have not been sleeping. I really need rest.

November 10, 1976

Life is so strange! Can you believe that I am having doubts about the move? What is the deal? Where is my head at? I am just so insecure about the future. I am used to guys hanging around and running around when I am single. I cannot imagine what it is going to be like this time, as a mother. I think getting right into school would really help. That would certainly change my lifestyle. I am so afraid that I am going to turn in one set of problems for another whole set of problems. What is the point? I do not want to end up alone. That is a real fear for me. I do not really want to move into Mom's flat either. So what is the big choice? One shitty situation for another. I just want to die and escape the whole thing. Was I just a fool to believe in love and happiness and peace? I cannot take all of this crappy unhappiness. What a shit, shit, shit life. I don't want any part of it except for my babies.

November 12, 1976

Isaiah 30:19-21

O My people in Jerusalem, you shall weep no more, for he will surely be gracious to you at the sound of your cry. He will answer you. Though he give you the bread of adversity and water of affliction, yet he will be with you to teach you, with your own eyes you will see your Teacher. And if you leave God's path and go astray, you will hear a Voice behind you say, "No, this is the way, walk here."

November 14, 1976

Today I feel like I have been speeding for a week. Mentally I am exhausted; physically my body is going 1,000 miles per hour. My stomach keeps cramping, I have had diarrhea and nausea for two days. Tomorrow!!! I am so glad, so sad, so scared and so nervous. Last night was Joshua's first birthday party. Everything went smoothly. Praise God, one down... Right before the party Tommy took at least twenty minutes to explain in detail how "fucking stupid" I am. All in front of Danialle. But I am supposed to teach her to be nice and not call people names. It is all so ridiculous and humiliating. Tomorrow!! For once Tommy will reap just what he has sown.

November 15, 1976

Dear Tommy,

Here goes the last letter that will be in your collection... We both know that this is the way that it has to be. I cannot stay here and be your whipping post, mental and physical. The person being hurt the most by my staying was you. Because you took it as my approval of what was done. But Tommy it's wrong, very wrong to abuse another person to the bizarre stage that the abuse went. Second, the only life Danialle and Joshua know is the life in the home. And they cannot grow up believing that they can abuse others or worse yet be abused by others. I pray Danialle's emotions have not already been affected by the things she has seen. No one should see in a lifetime the things that child has seen in three years. But I think I'm getting her away soon enough to overcome any damage that has already been done. Third, I was being destroyed completely as a person. I gave to you and gave to you until there was nothing left of me to give, not even a sound mind. You've treated me like some kind of animal. I forgive you Tommy but I no longer love you. So as far as you and I go, it is completely over. You'll just have to accept that. For once you're reaping what you've sown.

I've gotten a flat for us. I will contact you in a couple of days to arrange visiting time with Danialle and Joshua. If I ever find out that they have been exposed to any of your "tantrums," I will end all visiting privileges. They mean everything in the world to me and I will not let you hurt them emotionally anymore than what's already done. As long as you understand this, you can see them anytime you want. Although you'll be picking them up and dropping them off at my mother's. I will never be alone with you, as I've said, I'm afraid of you.

Do not cause a scene at my mother's today. I've already contacted the police and you will be picked up for trespassing if you go on her property without permission. Does this all seem cruel to you? Surely it's no crueler than beating a woman, especially right after childbirth and a difficult birth at that.

Good luck to you Tommy, you'll need it with your so-called "temper."

Gail

NOTE: After returning home and finding the note Tommy went to a restaurant where my girlfriend worked and caused a scene until she told him where we were. He came to the flat and started banging on the door and yelling for me to let him in "or else." I have never been so frightened in my life. I called the police for protection but back then they would not even come to the house because Tommy was legally my husband. I guess that made me his legal punching bag. I kept my children quiet as we sat huddled, crying on the bed while I read them books. I did not answer the door although I was tempted to because I was so accustomed to being intimidated by him. After what seemed to be an eternity, he gave up and left. Of course, I did not sleep for several nights for fear that he would break in and kill me. Surprisingly, after that initial incident his

Dr. Gail Majcher

threats became limited to phone calls, which were also quite frightening.

November 19, 1976

I am so happy for the first time in four years. I feel like the weight of hell has been lifted off my shoulders. The move went very smoothly on Monday. All Sunday night I lay awake wondering if Tommy was going to go to work or not. He left at 8:05 a.m., Mom and Janis arrived at 8:15 a.m., other friends arrived at 8:30 a.m. and the movers arrived at 9:00 a.m. We were completely out of there by 10:00 a.m. We didn't even talk, just sped around working. I couldn't talk, I was so nervous! So it went well. Of course, Tommy is freaking out. I could not care less. I am so glad to be out of there! I do not care for the first time in my life what anyone is saying.

I asked Pat if she thought that this traumatic event would force Tommy to face reality. She says that she doubts it because he is in a protective bubble. His family and friends acknowledge his "temper" as an idiosyncrasy rather than a sickness. Therefore, they can laugh and kid about it because it has been taken out of its right perspective. I know the truth; it is not just a "temper" but also a deep-rooted rage.

I now see things had to get to the bizarre extent that they did for me to look back with no regrets. The only thing I feel besides joy is pity. Pity for Tommy because I know how deep his problem goes and that he probably will never be helped.

I have realized that the most important thing in the world is peace of mind. I had been without it for four long years. I feel so safe, sane and secure. Something I have not experienced in so long. I am afraid about the future but I know we will make it and we will make it well. I now know the strength the Lord provides when you need it. I am so happy to be out. I love it. I love my place. It is so darling; it's like a dollhouse. I'm going to fix it up really neat. When I look back now it's like I was

62

living with a black veil surrounding me. Now suddenly, it's removed. The tremendous rage that I was ready to burst from is now gone. The move conquered that. I see how innocent and gullible I was to be the perfect victim in Tommy's family's game of "let's pretend." I tried living in a bizarre situation and pretending it was normal for their sake. But in the process, destroying myself. It is over now, only reality remains.

I know the divorce will be bitter because Tommy won't want to give me anything. But I do not care. I am just so glad to be out with my kids. They have adjusted tremendously well. I have been so busy and Danialle needs extra attention, we'll adjust. I find in life we have a way of doing and coping with whatever must be done. Healthy parents breed healthy children. I know that I am getting healthy therefore Danialle and Joshua will be healthy. I have to watch myself from talking about it all in front of Danialle. The sooner she can forget the events of the past, the better. I am so glad that we are out!

November 24, 1976

There is so much that I want to get written down. Cheryl, my best friend, suggested I get a tape recorder to record my thoughts. That is a great idea but I know I won't because I can't afford it right now. Today I don't even have enough money to get milk for the kids. I don't think anyone understands or cares about how poor I am. If I bought a tape recorder we would not be able to eat. This is so hard. I wish I had someone to help me financially. We will make it somehow.

My mind is going through so many changes I want to capture them all but I know that would be almost impossible. I have been experiencing so many emotions but the one I have not felt is regret. It is so strange because being the sentimental person I am; I usually get so hung up in the past. But for the first time in my life I am experiencing no regrets and no concern about what others are saying. Maybe I am in shock or something but I just do not care. Survival is much more important to me than people's opinions of my choices.

Tommy called today and told me how I had hurt him and how he deserves an apology. Once again, it is my fault. It just went in one ear and out the other. I do feel pity for him because I doubt that he will ever change. He just does not get it, even now after losing us.

One emotion I am feeling is fear. Fear that I am going to be alone the rest of my life. I know that there is no basis for this fear, I have only been gone a week but still I have to deal with it. I don't want to fall into a relationship just to fill the voids in my life. It's really a bizarre situation to adjust to. I never envisioned myself divorced, as a single parent. I never believed in divorce. Although Tommy and I had no type of relationship per se, he was a male in my life. I have always had a male in my life and being alone is very strange. Will I ever find my Rhett Butler? Do I need to? Can I find contentment without a man in my life? Is that possible? Can I make it financially without a man?

December 15, 1976

I was crying today asking God why this happened. How could it be that I am going to be a divorced woman with two children? Me, "Mrs. I don't believe in divorce"? How can I raise my children without a husband? What will become of them? How will I provide financially for us? What will Tommy do to me in court? Will he find a way to kill me yet? I suddenly felt impressed to read Isaiah 54. I didn't even know there was such a book in the Bible. I was amazed when I read it, God was answering my questions! Here it is: "...Break out into loud and joyful song, for she who was abandoned has more blessings (finances?) now than she whose husband stayed! (Tommy had emotionally abandoned me with the abuse)...Fear not; you will no longer live in shame. The shame of your youth and the sorrows of widowhood will be remembered no more, for your Creator will be your "husband" (an answer)...For the Lord has called you back from your grief...a young wife abandoned by her husband...My promise of peace for you will never be broken, says the Lord who has mercy upon you...And all your children shall be taught of the Lord; and great shall be the peace of your children (another answer)...Your enemies will stay far away, you will live in peace...no weapon formed against you shall succeed (another answer) and you will have justice against every courtroom lie (another answer)...This is the blessing I have given you, says the Lord."

Then I felt impressed to read Malachi 2:16. Who knew that this book was in there, too? It states: "Keep faith with the wife of your youth. For the Lord...says he hates divorce and cruel men." I now know that God hates that I have to go through the pain of divorce and He also hates what Tommy has done to me. I'll just mention one more scripture that came to me today. Hebrews 10:30 says: "Vengeance belongs to me, I will repay them, says the Lord." I am not to seek revenge on Tommy for the abuse I suffered. That is in the hands of God. I am not to repay evil with evil.

What an amazing day!!!!!!!!

February 7, 1977

Where do I begin? I have learned and been through so much in the past few months. Life still is not easy but it is better. My two biggest struggles are being alone and having no money. I am learning to like and appreciate me, which is a big step. I grew up with negative attitudes about myself and confirmed them by marrying someone like Tommy who is only capable of giving negatively. So now, with much conscious effort, I am beginning to like me.

If Tommy had never become physically abusive with me I

would have never left him. Tommy is not the man that is to be my husband. He began to break the marital bond way back on the honeymoon when he abandoned me by being mentally abusive to me. The physical abuse shattered the bond. It is no less of a breaking of the marriage vows than being unfaithful with another woman. Once the bond is broken, it is almost impossible to rebuild. All the kings' horses and all the kings' men cannot put it back together again.

March 7, 1977

You know, I have come a long way, baby. When I first left Tommy I felt so incomplete, so empty. I was so used to doing for another that I did not know how to function for me. That void was so strong; I wanted to have a man around to fill it. Now I see that it was a space within me that I needed to learn to fill. I had to learn to feel complete and satisfied with myself. And, you know, I did not even realize it was happening but, lo and behold, the void has lessened. I mean I am almost happy. That sounds funny but when you have been unhappy as long as I have, it is really a thrill to be almost happy. I mean on a constant basis, not just the ups and downs.

Tommy is trying to be real nice. He thinks that he has realized so many things. Maybe he has, but that does not mean it will change him. It is sad, but it is too late. He should have tried long before it reached this point because I just do not care. I do not want him. A couple of months ago when I had to go in the hospital for emergency knee surgery, Tommy threatened to get custody of the kids while I was immobilized. He said that he could do it on the grounds that I had abandoned them by being in the hospital. I became panic stricken until I talked to my attorney and he said that Tommy could not do that. How cruel. When the children cried for me while I was hospitalized he told them that I didn't want to see them. I don't want my babies to be with him, he uses them against me. Why do I have to make them go with him? Does this sound like a changed man? It will take much more than a few realizations for him to become healthy.

I see now that he will continue to be a painful thorn in my side in the years to come because the court gives him visitation rights. Why? He only harms all three of us emotionally. Danialle and Josh are doing so well with just me. I love them so much. It is hard being a single parent but easier than being with that crazy person. I wish we could be friends for the kids' sake, but he is not capable of being friends with a female.

August 4, 1977

As I look back over all that I have written, one page stands out and that is the letter I left Tommy. The reasons I gave him for my leaving were: 1. for his benefit; 2. for Danialle and Josh's benefit and, lastly; 3. for me. And you know that precisely represents how my life revolved at that time. Tommy was always number one, then the kids, then if any emotional energy was left, me. It is sad and ironic that I would put a man who abused me physically and mentally before myself. I have come a long way since then with many experiences both good and bad. Life is a constant learning process; rarely do we reach a plateau when we get to sit back and take a breather.

I have reached a slight plateau that I am very pleased about. After months of crawling and struggling inch by inch, I have come to a point where I am honestly liking and thinking about me. It is no longer what does everyone think of me. It is what do I think about them. And what do I want. This magnificent revelation has released a bondage within me, giving me a much greater capacity to love others. The old cliché of loving yourself before you can love others is very true. Unless you truly love yourself, you cannot honestly love others.

September 15, 1977

I am sure that I will go through many romances before I ever marry again, if I do. At this point it certainly is not anything I see or want in the near future. There are so many goals I have set and I think another person would only set me back. I want to make my mark while I am here. When I feel that a man is getting too close, I back off. I am glad; it's a good defense mechanism for where my life is at right now. If I do have a relationship with a man, it will be because I want it and how I feel comfortable, not only what he wants!! In other words it will be real, without all of the fantasies, because now I am pretty complete with just me.

October 10, 1977

Have I come such a long way? Sometimes I wonder. Maybe I am expecting too much, after all, growing and changing is generally a slow process. I am not as in touch with my feelings as I would like to be. I get so confused. Why do I put everyone else's needs before my own? What are my needs? I want to be so in touch with myself that I know what I think and feel at all times. I want to know without a doubt. I wonder if that is humanly possible. I wish I could call God; it would make life so much easier. Ha ha. The line would probably always be busy.

The area of mass confusion in my head is: Will I ever be able to trust a man enough again to feel safe enough to allow myself to care for him? I am so afraid of getting hurt. I think I have this fear because my emotions are not secure enough yet to handle any additional hurt. This is where the scars of the marriage lie. The abuse did so much damage to my ability to trust people. How does one overcome something that they do not fully understand? Part of me wants and needs love so much. I dream about someone, somewhere holding me and feeling so secure and content. But is that possible? Can I love

again?
    It is a hard life.

November 15, 1977
    One year since I left Tommy
What do I want?
I want freedom to do whatever I want, whenever I want.
I want to make my own decisions, even if they are wrong.
I want security, marriage, and a happy ever after.
I want to sleep with someone every night.
I want someone without insecurities that get put on me.
I want someone to share the joys of my children.
I want someone to share the burdens of my children.
I want to love someone.
I do not want to be hurt.
I want someone to calm my fears about life.
I want a relationship that I can walk away from.
I want a relationship where he would never walk away.
I want to get out of poverty.

    I am finally becoming me, as confusing as it all is. I thrive on it. I am learning who I am and loving it. Why do I still think about Tommy? Why can't I let go? What kind of bond forms when two people marry?

    Marriage meant so much to me. I want to share the joy and sorrow of parenting with him. I want him to be a normal father to my children. I loved our friends and his family. I loved our home. I loved his looks. I loved him. But I can let go and I am in the process. Tommy never realized that I was a person with feelings and thoughts. He thought that I was just an object he possessed. He tried to break my spirit but he couldn't. My spirit is a force stronger than my own conscious mind. It is the core of my being, the strength that keeps me going in spite of it all. My spirit is what keeps me standing no matter what life may throw at me.

June 1, 1979

Has so much time really gone by? It has not been easy, but there have been many blessings along the way. I am now in graduate school working on my master's degree in marriage and family counseling. Getting my bachelor's degree felt so good. I am beginning to feel worthy. Initially, going to college was very hard for me emotionally. The abuse made me so insecure that I became afraid of people in general. I went to my classes because I knew that I needed to, but many times I would cry on my way because I was so afraid. I think the fear was that I would be rejected and I just could not take any more rejection. It is amazing how much emotional damage was left from the abusive marriage. I have always loved being around people, now it scares me. But it is getting better. My peers have been friendly and supportive. That helps. They treat me like I am one of the brightest students. I'm beginning to feel like I belong. Accomplishing in school has played a major role in rebuilding my self-esteem. I meet interesting friends while school feeds my intellect as well as giving me a healthy focus. When life gets too hard I look to the future with my hopes and dreams.

I graduated with honors from the University of Michigan with my B.A. and now in graduate school I have a 4.0 G.P.A., it feels good. Who knew I had that ability within me? I put the kids to bed every night at eight and then study until midnight. It takes discipline but I am striving towards a goal that I definitely want to reach. I want to be able to provide a good home for Danialle and Joshua before they are old enough to know whether we are poor or not. They are definitely the joy of my life. When I feel beat up from all of my responsibilities I just look in their little faces to get renewed.

Danialle came home from kindergarten today with the results of a national test she took. She scored in the 97th percentile! She is a charming, articulate little girl with a wonderful sense of humor. She just shines. Joshua is a very joyful three year old. He loves to wait at the window for Danialle to come home from school each day. They love each other so much. Josh is about as lovable and huggable as they come.

I have not met that special man yet. But that's okay because my financial situation is so bad that I think it would be pretty darn tempting if someone asked me to marry him. And I don't think financial security is a good reason to marry. It is frightening walking the financial tightrope I live on. But I will not give up. I have been through too much to stop before my goals are reached. I want to become financially independent so I am never dependent on a man again in that way.

I am still in the process of being shaped, I have much to learn and a long way to go. And that is okay.

(This is the last entry to be published.)

The Aftermath

Chapter Five: ADC to Ph.D.

MANY YEARS LATER

From ADC to Ph.D. That is the title my mom thought I should use for this book. I know that she and my stepfather are proud of what I have accomplished and considering where I started, so am I. So the Ph.D. part is fine, but only someone who has been on welfare can appreciate the degrading feelings associated with receiving it. ADC stands for Aid for Dependent Children. It's called AFDC now. Welfare was not part of my family system and going on it to survive with my children was one of the worst experiences of my life.

It is difficult to explain the pervasive negative attitude that exists in our society towards anyone on welfare. Certainly it is a fact that many people abuse the system, but there are also many people who are using it as it was intended; for survival until they are able to get off of it.

I had to go to our local post office to get the food stamps to buy groceries so my children could eat. Now mind you, I was living in a middle to upper class suburb. Well, the emotionally bitter woman who gave out the food stamps found it necessary to degrade the people waiting for them. The stamps were only given out each day until 3:00 p.m. and you had better get there and wait in line by 1:00 p.m. whether there were two or twenty people in line. She would purposely dawdle so that at the cut-off time some people would be left hanging even if they had been waiting for hours. She did not care how many crying babies you had hanging off your hip.

One time I asked her why she was so nasty to people who were just trying to survive. She explained loudly that she could not stand people who lived off of the system. I guess she did not know she should not judge others and that she will reap what she sows. After being reduced to tears several times by her, I was starting to feel like a victim again. So I decided to take action and get the stamps at another location I could get in and out of quickly. Unfortunately, it was in a horrible part of town, an area where homicides were not at all unusual.

During one of my visits I locked my keys in my car. I was quite frightened when a disheveled man in a dirty trench coat, smoking something, approached me to offer his assistance. He pulled a long metal bar out from his inside pocket and quickly unlocked my car. As I stood amazed, he introduced himself as a professional car thief. Oh, my goodness. In retrospect, I realize that I must have been awfully naive about dangerous situations because I should not have been going to that part of town, especially alone. There must have been an army of angels surrounding me.

The grocery store was also humiliating because the cashiers would find it necessary to announce loudly when someone was using food stamps. The announcement triggered an outbreak of dirty looks from most people around me. The town where I lived was the same one I was raised in and where I had gone to school. Without fail there would always be someone in the store who knew me when this food stamp announcement was taking place and I don't think anyone ever pictured me to be the type to be on welfare. Nor did I. I was so embarrassed. It

was bad enough being a divorced, single mother without this added humiliation.

WHY WELFARE?

I was on ADC because after leaving Tommy I immediately went to college and began taking at least twenty credits a semester to get my degree quickly. Between that and raising Danialle and Josh there was no way I could work. Tommy was not about to be faithful with child support and never has been. Welfare was my only choice at that time. Tommy, like many men, never understood that child support was about financially supporting the children, not about giving me money. Noncustodial parents just don't get that child support is for supporting the children. It is not "giving" money to the ex-spouse. Whatever amount a parent pays in child support is typically only a small portion of what it really takes to support a child. I did not have an extended family to support me while I got my education or to help me raise my children. It was me, all alone, who had to figure out how to support and bring up my two babies.

When I first left Tommy I knew I had the option of going to work at Ford Motor Company, like everyone else in our city. For forty hours a week I could make a good living but it would mean leaving my babies in daycare. Or I could go to college, work towards a degree, suffer the humiliation of welfare but only leave my babies three days a week. That was the deciding factor. I was all they had and I could not bear the thought of leaving them in daycare for over forty hours a week away from me. They needed their mom and I needed to be with them. So there it was. I figured I could get my bachelor's degree in two to three years if I doubled up on credits per semester, then I could get a job.

Fortunately, the first year I was in school I became close, very close, friends with one of my psychology professors. It

was through my association with him that I realized I had it within me to not only go for my master's degree but also for my Ph.D. in psychology. I am grateful to him for enlightening me about academia. And for our weekly Saturday night dates to fabulous restaurants. On those nights I was not a welfare mom, struggling as a student, but rather I was transformed into Cinderella enjoying the world of the wealthy. Those times helped my self-esteem quite a bit given my life situation. But not all relationships are meant to last a lifetime.

HE'S BACK

So I got out of the violent marriage, went to college to become educated and began the awesome task of single parenting. My children and I were definitely on the road to a healthy life. Somehow I had not envisioned Tommy to be a part in this equation, but I was wrong. He had legal rights to the children yet he was the one unstable, irrational factor I could not remove from my children's life. I worked very hard to give them a stable, peaceful, loving home with safe, consistent boundaries. Tommy's form of parenting was diametrically opposed to what I was struggling to accomplish. Although he was capable of being a fun parent, the majority of the time Tommy was emotionally unavailable and unaware of what was appropriate behavior around the children.

For example, when Tommy was supposed to pick up the children at a specific time, I always had back-up plans for us in case he did not show up. This evolved out of watching my kids sitting by the window crying so many times when he "forgot" to pick them up. Sometimes this was not fair to me because I had made plans for myself when the children were gone. But I had learned by then that "fairness" did not apply to this relationship and never would. My children's needs took precedence over any issues of fairness. I also made sure that they had dimes to call me at anytime if they needed to. Back

then, beepers were not available but I think that they are a wonderful idea for mothers to have when their children go for visitation with an unstable father. My kids knew that if their father scared them, they were to call me. Sometimes they did and sometimes they were too frightened to.

It is extremely important for the children to know that their father's "temper" is not their fault. We would openly discuss the reality of the situation. Understanding his insecurities, character disorders, drug addictions or whatever didn't erase the pain, but it did help the children to see that it was his weakness causing the problem, not theirs. It is a problem inside of him even though they have to be exposed to it at times. It's not fair but that's the way it is.

When Tommy or his mother would make negative comments about me to the children, we would discuss it when they got home. I would explain why insecure people have a need to act this way. And that it was not our fault nor did we deserve it. My goodness, I was the only stable person my kids had, why would he and his family want to take that away from my children?

When I would beg Tommy to play ball with our son he would tell me to "shut the fuck up" and ignore Josh's needs. So I signed Josh up for every sport imaginable, sometimes he would enjoy it, sometimes not. Certainly having a dad involved would have helped, but you have to work with what you have. Danialle used to tell me that she would daydream about having a father, looking like a businessman, come to one of the many sport activities that she was involved in. I could not give her that but I could show up for all of the games and be an involved and proud parent.

One of the confusing issues my children had to adjust to with their father was that when he was being a "good" parent he was a lot of fun. Just like in the marriage, the hope is that he will continue to be this fun, loving parent on a consistent basis.

While he is being good, it is easy to deny that the negative side of the relationship even exists. But then there is the painful letdown when his personality shifts into the angry person.

Obviously getting out of an abusive marriage does not end the insanity. As long as there are children involved that person remains a part of your life for a very long time. Throughout the years Tommy continued to be verbally abusive to me whenever he got the opportunity and occasionally he would make feeble physical threats. Initially, he could push my buttons, but less so as time went on and I became more secure.

THAT ELEPHANT AGAIN

An incident occurred when the kids were in their early teens with Tommy getting angry about something on the phone with me; who knows what. A few minutes later I was inside the house, when I heard him drive up, get out of the car and tell the kids to stay outside. I felt panic run through my entire body. Although years had gone by, I found myself running into the bathroom and locking the door. He proceeded to barge into the house while yelling for me. I was frightened and shaking. I yelled through the bathroom door that I was in there and, how dare he break into my house. I told him to get out or I was going to call the police. He banged on the door, continued yelling profanities for a few minutes, and then he left. I just sat down and cried.

I could not believe this man could still bring such terror into my life so many years later. In retrospect, I realized I should have grabbed the cordless phone and called the police from the bathroom. But my first reaction when I saw him was to run for safety. For what it was worth, I filed a police report that day and he was no longer allowed to come within 500 feet of our home. So in spite of escaping from the marriage, his insanity still reared its ugly head at times.

HOPE SPRINGS ETERNAL

A few years ago I needed to call Tommy for the first time in a long time. In their teens, one of my kids was going through treatment because of a genetically inherited substance abuse problem. No matter who inherits the addiction gene, it affects everyone in the family. I realized through parent counseling that an addict has only three choices and that is to get sober, to go insane or to die. So I reached out to all resources I could think of to help my child. Tommy was one of the resources.

I called Tommy and asked him to please get sober and be a father during this period of treatment for the kids' sake. He told me to "shut the fuck up and stay the fuck out of his life." I hung up, looked at my husband and said, "Why do I bother?" I guess even now I continue to hope for some normalcy. Tommy has been cross-addicted to cocaine and alcohol for most of his life. For my children's sake, I hope he is able to get sober and work through his issues at some point in his life.

It was very hard to accept that one of my darling children had to fight the demons of addiction that were genetically passed down. With an alcoholic father and maternal grandfather, one of the kids was bound to inherit the problem. The genetics combined with the terrible teen substance abuse problem in this country was a lethal combination. My child's first experience with alcohol was at age four during visitation with their father who thought it was funny to see a child drunk. Needless to say, I was outraged.

At one point a woman, God bless her, at an Al-anon meeting (which I highly recommend) said to me that my children may have inherited a genetic weakness from their father. But it was the upbringing I gave them that provided the strength to control those demons. Those words were very healing to a mother who was wondering what she had done wrong and was heartbroken. When your child has a substance abuse problem, it is difficult not to assume the responsibility for it. And, of course, Tommy tried to blame me for this problem.

My child has now been sober and emotionally healthy for years and continues to actively work the twelve steps of A.A. I think if we all chose daily to work the twelve steps, we would have an incredibly healthy society. The steps are a practical, healthy guideline for everyone's life. They should be taught in middle schools to children across the country to promote sobriety.

MY BLESSINGS

I was blessed as a parent to have a daughter and son who have very similar personalities to mine. Consequently, I have had a good time raising them. As a matter of fact, to this day there is no one I enjoy being with more than Danialle and Josh. When I first started doing family therapy and heard horror stories from parents about their kids, I was shocked. Parenting was the one part of my life I felt I had a handle on. The rest of my life with school and work was very high pressure but not the parenting. Early on in my parenting experience I learned an excellent four step method of discipline, which worked well with my children and made our home peaceful. I have used this method successfully with hundreds of families in therapy. It is explained in detail in the last chapter.

This is not to say that single parenting was easy by any stretch of the imagination. No matter how good your children are or your discipline methods are, it is an extremely difficult task. There are definitely times when it feels like it is just too much for one person. I spent many hours crying over the stress of being a single parent. I just wanted someone, somewhere to help me. Yet so often when I would come home emotionally spent at the end of the day and see their little faces, my heart would melt and I would feel joy.

As a child, Danialle was articulate and funny; she could easily converse like an adult. She was, and is, the apple of my eye and my buddy. She is beautiful and very loving with a great sense of humor. We love to spend time together. Josh has always been the joy of my heart. He has a smile that just lights up a room. His teachers always commented to me about how special he is and, of course, I knew that. We have a great time hanging out (and working) together. He is the funniest person I know.

In spite of the enormous obstacles I had encountered as a single parent, my children have made it into adulthood in good shape. It does this mother's heart good to see where they are in their lives. Danialle is a professional writer, producer and model. She is even more beautiful inside than outside, which is saying an awful lot. Joshua is in college working towards a Ph.D. in psychology. He works as a psychotherapist and a school psychologist. He is an excellent therapist. They are both fine people of integrity, love and laughter.

Now that I have successfully raised my children into adulthood as a single parent, I have a few words of wisdom to pass on to parents. Most important, love your children enough to put thought and action into their well being. Make sure you assume the role as their protector. They did not choose to be born. You chose to have them so take that responsibility very seriously. They need to see ongoing acceptance and approval coming from your eyes. Give them at least four positive comments for every negative one. Set down the firm boundaries they need and be consistent which, at times, will be a sacrifice on your part. Children become insecure in gray areas; they need to know very clearly what is acceptable and what is not. Study the four-step method of discipline described in the last chapter of this book. Put it into practice. It does not matter what shortcomings the other parent has, one parent can do an effective job of parenting. Above all else, love your children in thought and deed. That covers a multitude of mistakes. Kiss them and hug them daily!

Chapter Six: Freedom

After completing my master's degree in marriage and family counseling, I realized that I needed to go on for a Ph.D. to support my children financially. In spite of intense competition, I was one of ten accepted into the Clinical and Educational Doctoral Program at the local university. Instead of being thrilled, I became depressed. I was tired of being in school and having no life other than studying and being mom. I did not want to do it anymore yet I knew I should feel honored I was accepted into the program. The internal conflict caused me to experience my first full-blown anxiety attack.

For weeks I prayed my heart out for direction about what was the best choice for me at this time in my life. I was open to whatever answer would restore my sense of well-being. One night some amazing truths were revealed to me that changed my attitude and goals. It was one of those "ah-ha" experiences where you suddenly have a very deep, clear understanding of something you have known for a long time. I realized that if anyone should be successful in life, it is those who have faith because we have tremendous power inside of us. We have the strength to move mountains with faith as tiny as a mustard seed. I had known and quoted that scripture verse for years, but that night I really understood it. It became alive to me. We can do tremendous works if we just have a little bit of faith. It is the insecurities within us that prevent us from accomplishing our goals and cause us to make excuses. Our lack of faith holds us back as we narrow our vision to focus on our shortcomings. We need to dream dreams and have visions.

Then I saw the reason we need to move up in this world's system is not for our egos but to reach more people with the love of God. The purpose of life is to give love to others. It is not about accumulating things and degrees. Along the road of success we benefit with finances and prestige but that should not be our main focus. I realized I needed to get my Ph.D. not for the financial benefits but to have the opportunity to minister love to more people. That was God's plan for me. Financial gains may come with the degree, but that was not to be my main focus. After that night there was no more anxiety about my decision. And those years in the doctoral program turned out to be hard work, but so much fun with a wonderful group of people, some who are still my closest friends today.

College is a good place for women to be when they leave an abusive situation. It provides a healthy focus on self and aids in planning the future. The sense of accomplishment that comes from earning a degree is so good for the self-esteem. And I found there is a way to get around some of the financial issues tied in with being a full time student. Each semester I would go to the library and look up books on scholarships and fellowships for women who were single parenting. You would be amazed by how many of these are offered each year. It was a hassle filling out all of the forms but the financial rewards of receiving some of these was well worth the effort. The money made life a tad bit easier.

By the time I completed school, I was in my thirties and, like many other woman at that age, I went blonde and a little wild, just a little. This is a stage many women go through that hits sometime in the thirties or forties. After all of those years of a strictly disciplined life with awesome responsibilities, I thrived on the feeling of freedom. I may not have had the title of Mrs. in this couples oriented society but I was now a "Dr." I was finally making decent money and my children's ages were in the double digits. And it felt good. I finally felt free to enjoy life. Next came the fabulous forties when many of my long term dreams finally came true. I look forward to the wisdom of the fifties. Life just keeps getting better. Who could have predicted that my "middle age" years would be so good after the horrific experiences in my twenties?

THE ENJOYMENT OF WORK

Some wonderful professional opportunities opened up for me, which just added to this good period. I started practicing therapy and was fortunate to quickly have a full caseload. This was quite amazing because typically it takes years for a new therapist to build up to a full caseload. But, at the time, I was one of the few therapists who dared to be labeled a "Christian" so I was the one local churches sent their people to see with their problems. I believe we are comprised of the body, the mind and the spirit and all three need to be addressed to aid in getting healthy. Fortunately, I realized I needed to spend much time in prayer as a new therapist for direction in how to help my clients. I believe God honored those prayers because I saw most of my client's lives change for the better. It is difficult to describe the feelings of gratitude I still feel as I observe this process of growth in my clients.

During this time I also began my career as a public speaker. Although I have spoken on a wide variety of topics through the years, my main focus has been on communication. So many issues can be overcome if we can communicate effectively. I remember the first time I was asked to speak in public. It was for a church and the topic was parenting issues. I spent countless hours preparing my presentation. When I arrived there were about a hundred people present waiting to hear me speak. I took one look at them and had to go into the ladies' restroom because I thought I was going to pass out from anxiety. It felt like my heart was going to pop out of my chest. But once I forced myself to go on stage and open my mouth, a calm took over and I enjoyed speaking. The only reason I continued to publicly speak back then was that I felt an obligation to if a church asked me. Now it is something I enjoy.

In addition to my well-established private practice, I had some other wonderful professional opportunities open up. In the early '80s, I worked as a mental health consultant for several Head Start Preschool Programs. Head Start is a preschool educational experience designed for low-income families. It is structured to give the children an opportunity to learn the skills necessary to be prepared for elementary school and to teach the parents how to parent effectively. It is a high quality government program. Working with Head Start was a gratifying experience for many reasons. I was able to work with single parents on welfare and help them to set goals for themselves they could see were realistic because of my own experience. I could truly empathize with their plight and teach them how to single parent effectively as well as move forward individually. Some of the single parents were ready to make changes; some were not.

I remember one time when I was conducting a parent training session for the parents at an inner city Head Start program. Several of the women got into a competitive dialogue about who had been abused more by their partners, not necessarily spouses. It was the wrong discussion to be having in my presence. As I confronted the issue, one of the woman said, "What would a white honky like you from the suburbs know about being beat up?" Well, you can just imagine their surprise as I shared my story.

I developed a wonderful relationship with those women and some of them started to view their own lives differently through the monthly parent sessions. The number of parents in attendance each month amazed me. Some began to have hope that things could be different if they wanted them to be. That was a healing period for me as I helped them and they helped me to recognize my own accomplishments. It was good for my self-esteem. And in addition, I was able to work with those darling little children. The preschool age is just so precious and it is the perfect time to give them a good head start on life.

I terminated my time with Head Start when I opened an adoption agency with a well-known attorney. That was a wonderful experience because, once again, I was working with children and parents. Helping couples to become families was truly one of the most gratifying experiences of my career. As an agency, we were changing laws about open adoption in our state and the notoriety and challenge associated with it was a great deal of fun. It was a period of high rolling socializing under the guise of work. It was a good place to be at that time in my life. I felt young and free for the first time since I was a teenager. Financially, I was more secure than I could have imagined a few years prior to this period. I finally had the freedom to do whatever I wanted. My children and I were able to go on many trips together and have numerous fun experiences.

THE DESIRE TO BE COUPLED

During these years I was single. And I am thankful for the time alone because I learned so much about myself and relationships through dating. Plus, I was able to fully devote myself to my children. But I really wanted to be in a healthy relationship. It was a challenge, wanting to be coupled but not finding the person that I could love and commit to. I could not settle for less than my whole heart and soul being committed to a man. So that meant waiting it out for years, maintaining hope and not settling in spite of temptations until I met the right person. There were a few false possibilities along the way that, thankfully, did not work out.

Sometimes I would try making bargains with God to speed things up but I guess His timing is perfect and not to be messed with. So in my long, long wait for my husband, Julius, I had many interesting relationships and experiences. With each man I dated I learned more about men and more about myself. In the process, I had an opportunity to work through a lot of my baggage from the abusive marriage.

Being in an abusive marriage leaves deep scars that need to be well healed or there is a risk of transferring them onto other relationships. For years when a man would reach for me to take my hand or put his arm around me, I would flinch. I immediately thought I was going to be hurt. During that time I found myself being a chameleon for men because I was afraid of the consequences if I dared to be myself. What a relief it was to work through that issue; being genuine is so freeing.

In therapy, I tell my clients to wait a year or two after a divorce before getting seriously involved with anyone. It is so important to take a period of time to heal. Many do not wait out of neediness, and guess what?

They end up in the same scenario that they just got out of. Remember the Lion that keeps rearing his ugly head until we face him head on? Same set up. Before we can be in a healthy relationship, we have to get healthy ourselves. We have to face the Lion.

It took me many years and many relationships before I had faced the Lion enough so that I could bring a healthy sense of self into my marriage. Those years were lonely. Even though I was not typically sitting at home staring at the walls, I had periods of doing just that. I knew it was bad when I started calling Peter Jennings my boyfriend because I watched him every night on television. I discovered many activities that kept my life fulfilled but I still longed to be coupled with the right person.

POWER IN PRAYER

Cheryl and I prayed Julius into existence, or so we believe. Through the years Cheryl and I have had many amazing answers to prayer. A month before Julius and I met, I was complaining to Cheryl about not having a date for all of the holiday parties coming up. So Cheryl and I agreed in prayer daily that God would send my helpmate to me, once and for all. Shortly before December, Julius appeared out of the blue. Don't you just love that name? The night we met at a restaurant I thought he was kidding, so I told him my name was Monique. Ha. Ha. After calling me Monique into the wee hours of the morning, I had to tell him that was not my real name. He had to know then that this was not going to be a normal, boring relationship. And it's not.

By the time I met Julius I was able to love him freely without expecting him to fill my voids. The fantasy expectations of my "husband" were gone and I could accept him for the reality of who he was; flaws and all, not that he has many. It had been sixteen years since I left the violent marriage when Julius and I met. Josh and Danialle were seventeen and nineteen. The long wait was good for my marriage for many reasons. One reason was that I gave up my subconscious expectation of Prince Charming. Many books have been written on the very real phenomenon called the Cinderella Complex. Many females from the baby boom generation unknowingly adopted it into their psychological makeup. It is the unrealistic expectation that the husband will miraculously solve all of the problems for the woman and make life magical. No one has that kind of power nor would we want him or her to. We have to work through our own issues and find our own happiness, independent of anyone else.

By the time I met Julius I had found my own happiness in life; most of it based around my spiritual beliefs, my children and my work. I am fortunate to be able to say I love my work. I have an unwavering belief that my clients have a healthy core covered up with unhealthy layers from childhood or other traumatic experiences. In the process of therapy we peel away those layers and get to the vibrant and beautiful inner self. Therapy is an amazing experience and it is difficult to describe the pleasure I feel as I see my clients grow. No matter where someone is emotionally when they come in, their lives can improve and become healthy.

Between my children, my work and social activities, my life was a gourmet main course; and Julius became the dessert. Dessert just happens to be my favorite part of the meal. I can say with conviction that Julius is my soul mate and I thank God every day for him. Sometimes I wake up in the middle of the night and am overwhelmed with gratitude for this man lying next to me. Does this mean we have no problems? Heavens no, nor would we want to be problem-free. Where would the growth be? We humans like status quo and we do not tend to move forward unless we get nudged a bit by life. Maintaining a happy, communicative marriage is a challenge. A challenge, but worth the effort invested.

SUMMARY

Well, that is my story thus far. I survived an abusive marriage, escaped and went forward against all odds. My children have grown into adulthood as secure, loving and productive individuals in spite of their violent father. We are living proof that an abused wife is not stuck in the cycle of insanity without choices. The choice to get out of the abusive relationship is a very real and viable option. I did it and so can you.

Against all odds, it is possible for a woman to escape from the abuse. We can overcome obstacles and move on to be victorious in our lives. We can rise above circumstances to find joy and peace while we move forward. Face those Lions in your life, run towards the roar and grow emotionally in the process. Let the inner you emerge, peel off those layers that keep you bound up. No matter what we encounter in our lives, let us always be able to say like, my buddy, Paul; "God has not given me a spirit of fear but of power and of love and a sound mind"(2 Timothy 1:7).

And above all else, do not let anyone abuse you. You may be a victim but you are not powerless, just look at my story. I got out, I am alive and I have a good life. You have the same strength within you.

May God bless you and keep you. May His angels surround you to keep you safe and whisper wisdom into your soul.

Part Two: Self Help
The Victim

Chapter Seven: Getting Safe

"...but God hath called us to peace." (I Corinthians 7:15b)

The American Medical Association defines domestic violence as an ongoing, debilitating experience of physical, psychological, and/or sexual abuse. According to the FBI, one out of every four women is a victim of domestic violence at least once in her lifetime. The Surgeon General of the United States reports that one out of five women are battered repeatedly by the same partner. In 55 percent of the cases, the children are also being abused. The leading cause of injury for women 15 to 44 is domestic violence. More women are killed at the hands of their partners than by strangers. Every 18 seconds a woman is being physically beaten by her significant other. Although both men and women can be the abusers, over 95 percent of the time the abusers are men. Domestic violence crosses all socioeconomic and racial barriers.

Violence is a curse overtaking our society. If we do not stop this insidious crime, our children and our children's children will die at the hands of violence. Fortunately, there is a way to stop this crime. We must begin to stop the violence by taking a look at our homes and ourselves. We must take all violence out of our own lives. Then we must take violence out of our homes. The home is the breeding ground for violence.

Domestic violence has passively been accepted as a norm in our culture. We know that it goes on but we do not want to deal with it. By closing our eyes to violence we are silently giving approval for its continuance. We say we care and we have compassion for the women, but we do nothing to stop it. This is not caring; it is only lip service to a crime that has such a wide reaching impact on our society.

This book focuses on women because in more than 95 percent of the domestic violence cases the victim is female. But abuse is not always about the male being the abuser. In my private practice I have seen a number of men who were being abused by their female partners. One of the primary issues with these men is that they are embarrassed to tell anyone they are accepting abuse from their wives. And when they do, no one believes them.

The bind that many of the men find themselves in is that they do not want to leave their children with an abusive person. They know there is a good chance that the abuse will not be believed in court and, therefore, they will not get custody. They spend a fortune trying to get full custody, but to no avail because the women do not look like "abusers." Many of the same issues that affect the abused women also affect the men. So if you are an abused male, this section will be beneficial for you. Abuse is never okay.

IS IT AN ABUSIVE RELATIONSHIP?

Many women do not think of themselves as being "abused" or "battered." They accept mental and physical abuse as the norm in their home. Somewhere along life's journey they have subconsciously learned to believe the lie that says they deserve to be abused. No women like it, but they accept it as their lot in life. They do not know they are women worthy of respect.

They are WORTHY WOMEN.

Excuses are made for the partner's violent behavior with the hope that it will be different in the future. Without that hope the woman has to make a decision for herself and her children. With the hope comes denial of the violence, as all remains status quo. The woman enables the partner in his unhealthy choices by accepting the abuse. It is the big pink elephant in the living room that no one talks about. When the violence is not acknowledged in an abusive relationship, everyone pretends it does not exist. If the woman does talk about it, she is treated like the crazy one and intimidated into keeping her mouth shut. Instead of the emphasis being on the abusive behavior, it is on the nerve of the victim for talking about it.

I believed that if I were the perfect wife and mother, then the physical and mental abuse would stop. I was wrong. The violence was within him; I had no control over it. Yet the dynamics of the relationship caused me to believe that it was my fault. If I talked about the violence, I was treated like I was the one that was doing something wrong. Fortunately, for my children and me, one day I woke up from the fog of denial and took action. This book is a wake up call to you. If you are not in an abusive relationship, you probably know someone who is. Take action for yourself or for them, it's the loving thing to do.

Listed below are questions to ask yourself. Answering "yes" to one or more indicates there is a problem in your relationship that needs to be addressed. None of the behaviors listed below are "normal" in a healthy relationship.

Has your partner...
Pushed, slapped, choked, hit or grabbed you?
Hit you with an object?
Left a bruise or wound on your body?
Threatened with or used a weapon against you?
Threatened to harm you or anyone you love?

Called you degrading names in public or private?
Forced you to have sex when you said "no"?
Forced you to engage in sexual acts you opposed?
Broken items or walls in anger?
Held you captive while screaming at you?
Put you down in front of the children or others?
Threatened to harm himself if you did something?
Scared you into doing what he wants?
Withheld transportation, money, food or medical attention?
Broken your personal possessions to hurt you?

If you answered "yes" to any of these questions, then you need to take a realistic look at your relationship. No one has the right to treat another person with this kind of cruelty. No one. Kindness and respect should be the norm in your relationship. If that sounds strange to you, then you need to turn your life around and get it on a healthy track. You do not need someone in your life that is trying to control you. Abuse is about one person trying to control another with fear. Domestic violence is always a control issue.

My favorite Shakespearean play is the "Taming of the Shrew." The woman, the shrew, was a feisty character that her father could not handle. He offered a reward for anyone who could tame the shrew. Most men tried to control her with cruelty, but a stranger approached her in a different way. He took her away and treated her with kindness. It was through kindness he tamed the shrew. The main emphasis of the play is that we develop good relationships through kindness not through abuse. Ongoing kindness should be the norm in ALL relationships. Battering is NEVER okay. Being controlled by another person is not healthy. You need to believe that abuse is NEVER okay. And, you are not alone with this problem. There is help available for you.

THE TYPICAL CYCLE

The typical cycle of violence is four-fold. First, there is the calm phase. No abuse is taking place, past incidents are forgotten and the victim slips into her hopeful state. Then the tension starts building with mild abuse beginning while the victim starts trying to placate the abuser. Next, it is time again for the physical, verbal, emotional and/or sexual abuse to occur. Lastly, the reconciliation phase starts as the abuser is remorseful and swears that either he did not do it or that he will not do it again.

The length and intensity of each stage varies in each relationship from hours to months. The abuse tends to escalate in frequency and intensity with time. At some point the calm and reconciliation phases may begin to fade out as the tension level increases to an ongoing, unbearable level.

STEPS TO SAFETY

If you are in a domestic violence situation, you do have options. Help is available for you. You can create a safe, peaceful home environment for yourself and your children. That may sound like wishful thinking at this point, but it is true. Listed below are several suggestions for immediate action to change your life.

A. Call the National Domestic Violence Hotline at 1-800-799-SAFE. Tell them about your situation and ask for phone numbers of domestic violence shelters in your area. Shelters are comprised of caring, compassionate people who have a wealth of information you need to get yourself safe. Find out what services they offer and how they can help you. All of the interactions are kept strictly confidential. You are not committing to leaving or ending a relationship by making a phone call.

Call a shelter for information even if you need to disguise

your name and voice to feel comfortable, or have a trusted friend call for you. I wish these wonderful shelters were in existence when I was an abused wife, it would have made the escape much easier. I would have been thrilled to find someone to talk to who really understood what I was going through, a person who would not blame me. Most people I confided in acted like I was fabricating the abuse because they did not understand it.

B. Call the police. The police exist to protect us. Do not be afraid or embarrassed to call them for help. Have their emergency phone number memorized. If you do not have a phone, have a signal for neighbors to call the police, if necessary. When the police arrive it is extremely important that you are very specific about what has occurred.

This is NOT the time to get hysterical and, please, do not take your anger out on the police if they happen to be male. The police are on your side and you want to treat them as your support system. Most police officers have some training in the dynamics of domestic violence. They know what can be done to help you.

Describe the abuse; show them the wounds and any broken items around the house. If it is possible, talk to them in private so your partner does not intimidate you. The police can protect you from immediate harm. If they are clearly shown there was abuse, they can arrest the abuser. Do not fear the arrest, it can give you time to get to safety. Besides, your partner needs to know there are consequences attached to abusing another person. Make sure a police report is written. You may want to use it in the future for a Personal Protection Order.

C. Get support from family and friends if they are "safe." Some family and friends have a vested interest in using denial to ignore the violence. They are not "safe." Determine if you have any supportive people in your life who will believe you and who care enough to take action if necessary. If they diminish the severity of what is occurring, they are not safe. Safe people believe you and want to help in any way possible.

Tell your supportive people about what has taken place. Talk openly with detail about the abuse. You need to voice it and they need to hear it. This is a good step in facing the reality of the situation and not assuming responsibility for abuse. Remember that the abuse is within him. No matter what you may have done, violent behavior is NOT a normal reaction. Battering is NEVER okay. You are not responsible for the abuse. At this point you do need to assume responsibility for getting you and your children into a safe environment. This is healthy responsibility.

D. Find a safe place of escape. This may take some time and effort so you want to be working on this now. One of the many unfair issues about domestic violence is that the victim is usually the one who must leave the home to find safety. This is unfair and it is not right, but it is the way it is. And when the issue is abuse, it is more important to get safe than to take a stand for what is fair. You can fight for fairness after you get out and are safe.

Shelters throughout the country can help you to relocate. If you have the finances, get an apartment to escape to with your children. It is a good transitional place to be. Perhaps you have "safe" family or friends you would want to stay with for a while. Do NOT let the abuser know where you are going. Many women are murdered after they leave the abusive relationship. If you are not ready to leave, find a safe place you know you can go to at a moments notice.

It took me about two months to get everything in order to move into a safe place. Back then there were no shelters and no one wanted to rent to a single mother on welfare. So I had to talk my mother into letting me move into a flat she owned. It was a hard thing to do, but it is amazing how much strength you develop when you fear for the safety of yourself and your children. Initially, I had to go on welfare to have money for rent and living expenses. Although it was not much, it was enough to survive. If you do need to go on welfare, make a goal to get off it as soon as possible. Existence on welfare is not good for anyone's self-esteem. Being a productive member of society is very good for one's sense of self.

E. Get medical attention. If you have been physically abused, go get medical help at an emergency room or urgent care unit immediately. You do not know how severe the damage is. You may have injuries not visible such as internal bleeding or a closed head injury caused by a blow to the head.

Tell the doctor exactly what happened. Do not hide the truth from the doctor. You cannot get appropriate help if you distort what took place. Do not let embarrassment stop you from getting proper medical treatment. Most medical facilities now have supportive people trained in domestic violence who can be helpful to you. Get as much information from each knowledgeable person as you can.

The more information you have, the better equipped you will be when it is time to leave. Medical records about the abuse can help you in the future with a personal protection order or a civil court case. This is another reason to be truthful and precise when you are explaining to the doctor what happened to you. The medical records may also be helpful to you when it comes time to deal with visitation and custody issues.

F. Get a Personal Protection Order (PPO). A PPO is an order issued by the court to protect you from anyone who has physically, emotionally or sexually abused you. Stalkers are also included in this protection order. It can protect you from harassment, threats, assault, beating, molesting or stalking by another person. The violator will not be allowed to come near you no matter where you are. He will not be allowed to enter your premises nor go to your place of employment. Visitation arrangements for your children will need to be changed to a new location away from the home.

Call your County Clerk's Office to get accurate information about how to obtain a PPO in your state and what you need to do and bring. Take as much information as you can about the abuse and the abuser and any court documents you have with you. Bring photographs and any other good descriptive information. The process may take a couple of hours, but it well worth the time. Many women's lives have been saved because they had a PPO. The PPO is effective as soon as the judge signs it. The abuser will be served with the order. Carry it with you at all times. Unfortunately, many women will take the time to get a PPO, but will not follow through on calling the police when the violator breaks the order by coming near the victim. PPO's can be very effective but only if you choose to use them.

G. Make a personalized safety plan. Take the suggestions that have been listed and make a plan for you and your children. It is helpful to develop the plan with a counselor from a shelter, a therapist or a supportive friend although you can do it alone. This safety plan is about saving your life and the lives of your children. Your safety is important for survival.

❋ KEY ISSUE: TAKE YOUR CHILDREN WITH YOU

Make sure you take your children with you. Everything else is secondary. Get legal custody of your children within a couple of days. Call the Friend of the Court in your county for advice. You need to have the children with you to do this. Listed below are important steps you want to include in your safety plan.

1. Have the phone numbers of the police, an emergency hotline, a shelter, and friends written down for you and your children. Keep these numbers with you at all times. Memorize them if you can.

2. Tell your "safe" neighbors or friends about the violence. Ask them to call the police if they hear any suspicious noises coming from your house or if they notice anything odd.

3. Figure out at least four places where you can quickly go for safety. Memorize the quickest, most direct route to each destination. If you do not have a car to use, determine how you will get to your safe place. There is always a way if you want it bad enough.

4. Put together a package of extra money, home and car keys, clothing, medication and important papers to give to a safe friend. If this plan seems dramatic to you, keep in mind more than half the women murdered in this country are murdered by their partners.

5. Keep money on you at all times for phone calls or get a phone card and memorize the card number. Open a savings account in your name and put some money in it. It can be only a few dollars to begin with. No matter how much money you are able to stash away if you need to leave, it will be helpful.

6. Figure out how you will get out of the house during or after an abusive episode. Some woman go out to get the newspaper, have a cigarette, get something from the car, walk the dog or whatever. Decide what you can use as an excuse that is part of your regular routine. Create a new part to your routine, if necessary, to have an out to escape or at least make a phone call. If you have a cellular phone, keep it somewhere accessible yet discreet.

7. Review and rehearse your safety plan on a regular basis.

Review it with a safe person. Let the plan become very familiar to you and to another person.

H. Remove or lock up any weapons in the house. If the weapons can be removed, do so immediately. If you cannot remove them, determine if you can remove the ammunition. You are doing this to protect your life and the lives of your children. One-third of all assaults involve a weapon. When a person is out of control, you do not know what they are capable of doing. If the weapons are illegal, take them to the police. Do not minimize the significance of removing the weapons. They are dangerous.

SUMMARY

Please take the time to carefully read these steps to safety. Your life and your children's lives are at stake. Women are murdered daily by their abusive partners. Domestic violence is a life-threatening problem. Do not downplay the violence because it is happening to you. You do not deserve to be abused. No one does. It is wrong. If you continue living in the violence with your children, you will all become damaged emotionally or worse. Get yourself and your children to a place of safety. That does not mean that your relationship is over. It means you are taking a stand to protect you and your children. You are taking a stand for your sanity and safety. It is a difficult thing to do, but not as hard as the consequences of being abused.

Chapter Eight: Staying Safe

If you choose to leave the abusive relationship, there are some precautions you need to take to make sure that you stay safe. The danger does not end when you walk out the door. Many women are murdered after they leave the abusive relationship. Listed below are some steps for staying safe after the relationship is over.

STEPS TO STAY SAFE
A. Change the locks on the doors no matter where you end up living. You do not know who has access to those keys. If possible, install steel doors that are difficult to break down. Put in deadbolt locks. Have a security system installed.

When I left, I bought a simple little alarm from the drug store that I attached to the door (an electric screwdriver can become a woman's best friend.) If it was turned on and the buzzer went off, I knew someone was opening the door. It was all I could afford and it offered me some protection. Make sure your smoke detectors are working. Get the motion-sensor light bulbs for all outdoor lighting or leave outdoor lights on all night. Having one of those small personal alarms on you or near you at all times may make you feel a bit safer. They are inexpensive and when the pin is pulled it makes a very loud, shrill sound.

B. Let your neighbors know about the situation. Show them a picture of the abuser. Tell them you have a personal protection order. In this case it does not matter if they really understand domestic violence or not. Ask them to call the police and you immediately if they see the abuser anywhere near your place of residence. Reassure them they are not in danger, but you may be. This is not being dramatic. This is facing the fact that so many victims are brutalized after they leave. Have your neighbors' phone numbers on hand in case of emergency.

C. Tell the school and the people who take care of your children who is and who is not allowed to pick them up. Have the caretaker and/or school write down the names of whom your children can be released to. Repeat the names to be certain that it is clearly understood. Do not assume anything. Some batterers are very charming people and do not appear to be the "type" to abuse their partners. Educators and babysitters can be fooled just like you were. Even educated women get abused. If you have a PPO, make copies to give to the caretakers and the schools. Your partner may try to kidnap or harm the children in an attempt to get you to return to him.

D. Inform someone at work about the situation. You and the police need to be notified if the abuser shows up at your place of employment. Do not be surprised if you have a few odd altercations at your work. Your abuser may want you to lose your job so you will need him to support you. If possible, ask that your phone calls at work be screened for a period of time. Harassment at work is a violation of the personal protection order; take advantage of this for your safety.

E. Change your daily routine. Now is the time to change your bank, grocery store, cleaners, and other businesses that are part of your routine. View it as an adventure as you try out new places to do your business. It is time to create new patterns that will have memories of safety and peace. Change the route to your work and your children's school. If possible, change the times that you previously departed for each location. For example, leave early and stop and get a bagel and juice in the morning; the kids will love it. Change is necessary.

F. Develop a short list of people for emotional support. Leaving an abusive relationship is such a difficult thing to do. It takes so much emotional energy. You will need to rely on others at times to help pull you up. This is an area where therapy or support groups can help keep you centered. Support groups can also be a good way to develop new friendships.

At times you will feel like giving up and going back with the abuser. We are creatures of habit and we resist change. Even if the habitual behavior was unhealthy for us, we are drawn back to it because it is familiar. I remember having days, weeks, months of such deep sadness that I felt like I could hardly get out of bed. At times I would cry for days. It's called grief and it is normal. This is the time to rely on friends for support. There is something very therapeutic and comforting about voicing our feelings to another. Our vision can become cloudy when we are in pain. Safe friends can help us to stay focused and balanced in our thinking.

It is very sad to give up a relationship you thought would last forever. With time, the grief lessens. Time does heal all wounds. Close friends can help speed up this process with their love and support. I am still sad at times that I was not able to raise my children with their biological father. Yet how damaging it would have been for us emotionally if I had given in, again, and gone back to the abuse. I have no doubt that at

EVERY BATTERED WOMAN'S HOPE

There is an interesting phenomenon that may occur when a woman finally reaches the point of seeking therapy while she is still in the relationship. The man becomes threatened because his wife is taking a stand and getting help. Remember abuse is always about control and this therapy thing is not in the abusive partner's control. He may react in one of three ways. One, the violence may increase as he tries to gain back control of your life, so be prepared with your safety plan. Two, he may want to come to therapy in an attempt to placate you and to control what takes place in therapy. Three, he may want to come to therapy because he would rather learn how to work through his rage than lose you.

This third reaction is the ideal, but rarely happens. Yet rare as it is, I have seen men genuinely work hard to overcome the violent tendencies within themselves rather than face losing their partner.

The therapy is done with the understanding that if any form of abuse happens again, the relationship is over. The therapy is very difficult for the man as he takes a realistic look at what he's done to his wife and children. It is extremely painful to let go of the defense of denial. The therapy takes a long time. As he begins to heal he also has to accept the anger his spouse has towards him. It takes a long time for the wall of mistrust to come down. That wall is a safety net for the woman and it does not come down until she can trust that he is no longer abusive in any form. Let me repeat, this choice for change rarely happens.

This reaction of legitimate change is what all battered women hope for, but rarely get. And the only hope for this change is when the woman takes a firm stand to get help and no longer accepts abuse. Enabling love does not work, but sometimes tough love does. An abusive man does not need a partner who allows herself to be abused. That is the kiss of death for both of them emotionally. He needs someone who respects herself enough to say, "No more abuse" even if that means leaving him. Tough love can be effective. We need to take a firm stand by refusing to accept the unhealthy choices of those we love. It is a difficult thing to do, but it has proven to be the one act on our part that sometimes gets results. But sometimes nothing works because we cannot change another person's will. My spouse came to therapy during one of my attempts at getting help. He wanted to control the session and he succeeded. Unfortunately, that therapist was a student intern and had no clue as to what domestic violence was all about and it did more harm than good. Check on the therapist's experience.

My spouse did not bother getting involved the last time I got therapy while in the marriage. He just called me the "crazy" one because I needed a "shrink." He openly shared that bit of information with anyone who would listen. (Little did he know that one day I would end up leaving him and becoming a therapist!)

H. Spend some time each day in prayer and/or meditation. Many times it is our relationship with God (or our Higher Power) that keeps us sane through these difficult times in life. Through prayer and meditation we can transcend to a place that gives us peace that passes all understanding. It is in this spiritual state that we become strengthened enough to handle making the decisions necessary to get out of a domestic violence situation.

I believed that God wanted positive things for my life and that He had a good plan for me in spite of the mess my life had become. I was right. After I got out of the abusive relationship, my life took a dramatic swing for the good and, in spite of minor setbacks, it has continued in that direction. There is no doubt in my mind that it was by God's grace that I got out and went on to have a good life. Our responsibility to ourselves is to choose to stay spiritually focused and safe. It is a gift we give to ourselves.

I. Recognize that loneliness is okay. It seems to be a normal human tendency to fear being alone. People stay in unhealthy relationships because of this fear. Many women return to abusive situations after leaving for this reason. I did, numerous times. Yet being alone is not so bad. Actually it has many good features that I learned to enjoy and appreciate. Being alone for many years gave me an opportunity to really get to know who I am. I learned to recognize my strengths and my weaknesses and truly be okay with each. Depending on just me helped my self-esteem develop to a healthy level.

But it took some time after I left the marriage to adjust to being a single person without another adult in my life. Initially, I had periods of extreme loneliness that were hard to cope with until I had a realization one day. I remembered vividly that I was lonely and very sad throughout my marriage. I realized in reality I was far less lonely being single than being married. Odd.

I developed a routine for dealing with those times of loneliness. I found that some of the loneliest times would be when my children went for overnight visitation with their father. I learned to use the time to pamper myself by doing things I would not normally do. Sometimes I would go see two movies at a time or buy a nice, thick romantic novel to get entrenched in or I would spend the night at a girlfriend's home or I would prepare a special meal for myself or I would just enjoy the solitude and reevaluate my goals and my ideals or I would spend time building my spiritual life. It is a good idea to keep an ongoing list of things you would like to do when you are feeling lonely.

If I had my children with me and I was going through a

lonely period, I would plan special activities for us. I called these events a "journey" and the kids would get all excited when I would say that we were going on one. Most of the time they would be a spur of the moment idea. A lunch in the park or a trip to the zoo or walking around a neighboring city are just a few of the many fun distractions for loneliness. Those sad feelings can be the inspiration for some wonderful experiences for you and the children.

SUMMARY

You are a Worthy Woman. You deserve to be safe and to live without fear. A proactive approach to safety is necessary, especially at this time in your life. You must take the necessary precautions to keep you and your children free from harm. The steps listed are for your protection, but only you can activate them. Show yourself respect by securing all protection possible. You and your children deserve the energy and effort it takes to be safe.

And let the loneliness be a time of growth for you. When I did not have someone to do special little things for me, I did them for myself. It became an opportunity for learning how to take care of myself and learning to value my own feelings. At some point I finally recognized I was worthy of any special attention given to me by others or myself. I learned to expect and tolerate only respectful treatment from others. In retrospect, I realize the time I had of being alone was an invaluable time of growth for me. Let it be the same for you. Being alone is okay, it can be a good thing.

Chapter Nine: Getting Emotionally Safe

It is not possible to maintain a healthy self-esteem while being abused. Emotional, verbal, physical and/or sexual abuse opposes feelings of self worth. Consequently, there is always a need to work on feelings of low self-esteem when abuse has occurred. If people allow themselves to be abused on a continuous basis, there is a need to look within to figure out why this treatment has been accepted. More often than not it is an issue of poor self-esteem originating from shame.

SHAME
Shame is the emotional feeling way deep inside that tells you there is something wrong with you although there is no rhyme or reason for that belief. It is an ongoing feeling that somehow you are not as good, intelligent, attractive, normal or whatever as other people. We all have moments of these feelings, but shame is different because it is ongoing. It is a deep unspoken yet present belief about one's self. Shame does not say, "I made a mistake," it says "there is something wrong with me."

These feelings of shame do not allow a healthy self-esteem

to develop. Outwardly a person may appear totally "together" but it is only a false self if shame exists within. Shame allows a person to accept abuse because deep inside is the mistaken belief that for some unknown reason they may deserve the punishment. People with a healthy self-esteem would not allow ongoing abuse in their lives. They would not even think of tolerating an abusive relationship.

People living in shame make excuses for other people's inappropriate behavior toward them while subtly assuming the responsibility for whatever conflicts exist. They enable others to act wrongly by not taking a stand for what is right. Good mental health is based in reality and living with shame causes one to distort the reality. Sounds a lot like codependency, doesn't it? Yep, here it is, rearing its ugly head again. Many people who battle the negative feelings of shame exhibit codependent tendencies, while others may exhibit controlling behavior such as being the abuser. Abuse and codependency are two sides of the same coin. People tend to gravitate to a partner who is at the same psychological level they are. Shame may be the root cause of both the abusive behavior by the abuser and the acceptance of it by the victim.

This reminds me of a quick story concerning my nephew, Sammy. When he was about four years old he was acting up at the dinner table. My sister said to him, "Shame on you, Sammy!" And he, very innocently, looked around and said "But, Mommy, there's no shame on me." Don't you love that? If only we could all have that same attitude! No, there is no shame on us.

DEVELOPING A HEALTHY SELF ESTEEM

The initial step to becoming emotionally safe from ever accepting abuse again is to develop a healthy self-esteem. Counseling, supportive friends, support groups, and strengthening our relationship with God are the best ways to learn to value ourselves. Make those a top priority in your life. In addition, there are various techniques you can incorporate into your everyday life that will start to raise your self-esteem and erase the shame. Listed below are six precise steps to follow to aid in the self-esteem building process.

STEP ONE

First, identify those negative, shameful feelings within you. Write about them daily in a journal so you become consciously aware of the feelings and thoughts associated with shame. Do not fight them during this period but understand them so you know what it is you are going to work on. You cannot have victory if you are not consciously aware of the shame.

Write down all of the negative beliefs you have about yourself no matter how ridiculous they may appear to be. Write down at least five that play over and over. Become familiar with the negative messages that are played out in your mind. They are lies, they are not true. Somewhere within your healthy self, you know that. Your authentic self, which you were born with, is covered up with layers of these untrue, negative messages. It is now time to start to peel those negative messages off and get down to the real you that feels good about yourself. You probably learned the negative beliefs about self in childhood. We all learn some negative messages, but to varying degrees. We do not need to blame anyone for giving us these messages; we just need to get rid of them.

STEP TWO

Second, you are going to learn to replace these negative thoughts with some easy techniques that are quite simple. Next to each negative statement written on your list put down five positive ones about yourself. You do not have to believe the positive statements at this point. That will come with time. Remember the title of this book and include "worthy" statements with your positive affirmations. Keep this journal in a private place so you do not have to be concerned who might read it. Here are two examples of some of the common shame messages:

Negative: I am ugly and fat.
Positive: God has blessed me with beautiful eyes.
I am thankful for my healthy body.
I have smooth skin.
I am blessed with the sense of taste that allows me to enjoy food. My worth and respect are based on who I am inside.
Negative: I say stupid things.
Positive: I am so grateful that I have vocal cords that work.
It is good for me to voice my opinion.
I have important things to say.
I have a good mind.
I have been created as an intelligent, worthwhile person.

STEP THREE

Step three, now comes the difficult part. It is difficult because it takes energy. We can learn techniques in many areas of functioning, which would benefit our lives, yet we let days, weeks, months go by without doing them. Each day we know we should work out and eat healthy but do we? Self-help techniques, by definition, only work if we help ourselves. In therapy I have many of my clients do homework activities to speed along their progress. Yet some will come in sheepishly each week because they did not do them. I understand it is easier to do nothing, but that's exactly what we get, nothing. For self-help techniques to work, you must apply them.

This step takes some energy to put it into action. Four times each day give yourself five minutes to read out loud each positive statement, not the negative ones. As you are speaking each one, visualize what you are saying. If you are saying that you have smooth skin, then get a picture of that skin in your mind's eye. You do not have to believe each positive statement, just make sure you voice it. There is amazing power in the spoken word. We must be very careful about what we voice because there is a good chance it will come true. Practice voicing positives in all areas of your life. It is so healthy for you and it will help create positives in your life.

It is important to do the positive affirmations for at least four weeks, if not indefinitely. It takes at least three weeks to break a negative habit. Do you know that most people attempting to get sober on their own can typically maintain sobriety for three weeks? We are creatures of habit and after about three weeks it is very easy to slip back into the old unhealthy patterns. Many abusers can stop being violent for the same amount of time.

Those negative thoughts are just an old habitual way of thinking. The good news is that we can change our thought patterns. It's called cognitive restructuring. That is such a wonderful term. It is a great feeling when you realize you really do have the power to restructure your cognitive (thought) patterns. The positive affirmation technique is one of many ways to build your self-esteem and is quite effective if applied daily, like anti-wrinkle cream. Once a month revamp your list by going through the first three steps.

You can involve other people in your positive affirmations but only if they are safe. A close, supportive friend can do them with you sometimes and encourage you to believe what you are saying. Have your friend also make a list of her own affirmations.

Children are wonderful to do affirmations with and you will be teaching them an invaluable life lesson about being positive. If your children have been exposed to abuse in the home, they need as much positive input in their lives as possible. At dinner my children and I used to say three positive statements about each other while we ate. It felt good and it helped to create a sense of support towards each other that still exists today. Sometimes the positive statements would be hilarious and silly, but that's okay. It is important to train our children to be positive about themselves, their siblings and us. Many times children from abusive homes develop a negative attitude problem from the abused parent. This is a good activity to change that learned negative attitude.

STEP FOUR

The fourth step in this self-esteem building technique is to start saying the affirmations to yourself in the mirror. At first it will feel weird. Many people who are dealing with shame do not like to look at themselves in the mirror. It is important to look at yourself and learn to feel good in your own skin. Look at that person in the mirror and become friends with her. That person you see is the one that you want to learn to love. She is A WORTHY WOMAN. She is worthy of your love and she needs it.

STEP FIVE

In doing therapy for so many years; I have spent countless hours thinking about this issue of self-esteem. There are many approaches to creating a healthy sense of self and I believe that this fifth step is one, if not the primary, key to creating a rock solid self-esteem. To feel secure, we need clear principles by which we try to live our lives. These principles need to be so clear and solid within us that we know that whatever is happening externally, internally we are people of integrity.

This week I had a client in therapy that is struggling emotionally because his wife of many years wants to divorce him. Through his tears he asked me a personal question. He said, "After all you have been through with the abuse and divorce and all, how can you have a healthy self-esteem?" Great question. Without thinking I responded, "My self-esteem comes from knowing that no matter what situation I have found myself in, I know that I was trying to live a life that would be pleasing to my God." I have attempted to make choices with integrity although sometimes I have totally blown it. My self-esteem does not come from the external, which is temporal, but rather from my internal attempt to be virtuous.

There are basic spiritual principles that just sit right with every one of us. We function best and feel the best when we are trying to live a life based on these principles. I found my principles by studying the Bible. I view the Bible as a handbook on how to live life to the fullest. Everyone must do it in his or her own way. In the search for truth we all come to the same road with similar truths about what is good for us and what is not. Truth is truth no matter where you find it. So search out what your life principles are. Write them down. Read books and listen to tapes. Educate yourself about good, healthy principles in life.

STEP SIX

This is a difficult step. We must forgive the abuser. Forgiveness is one of the key issues in promoting our own mental and physical health. When we hold on to the pain of abuse, we are choosing to not let our minds and bodies be at ease. These are ripe conditions for disease (lack of ease) to enter in, either physical or mental. The anger and bitterness associated with not forgiving works against us. God knows the abuse has created enough stress in our lives without letting it continue once we are safe. At least forgiveness is something we have control over.

Forgiveness does not mean forgetting about what has occurred and/or letting our guard done. It means allowing ourselves to identify and feel our feelings. Then it is a conscious choice to stop focusing on the pain and let it go. Our focus needs to be on healthier issues. Only then are we ready to forgive the abuser for what he has done to us. Genuine forgiveness can take months or years to accomplish. It is not easy when you have been abused.

REAP AND SOW

There is a spiritual law that can aid in the process of forgiveness. People reap what they sow in life. Victims do not need to waste time seeking vengeance against the abusers because they will somehow, someday get caught in their own folly. It is not possible to come out the winner if we attempt to fight violence with violence.

We have to take a stand by getting away from the violence and making ourselves safe. Then the legal system can be used to seek out justice. Though there are inherent flaws in the legal system in regards to domestic violence, we should use it to whatever extent possible to make our partner responsible for the abuse.

I have seen the spiritual law of sowing and reaping come to pass over and over again in many people's lives. For example, shortly after I left Tommy, he got in a brawl with a couple of policeman who beat him up, leaving a scar on his face. He was reaping just a tad of the violence he had sown. I have seen him reap it repeatedly throughout the years. His life has not been a good one. He has never remarried and he has been a drug addict for most of his adult life. I do not take joy in seeing his pain; it brings me great sadness. I loved Tommy at one time and saw the tremendous potential he had and it grieves me to see the direction that his life took.

When I was married to him, I called his father at work one day and begged him to intervene concerning the abuse, but he said, "When you married him, he became your problem." What a cruel statement to make to a bruised, pregnant 22 year old battered wife with a toddler. On our wedding day, his father had remarked to Tommy's cousin "It will be a miracle if this marriage works." Even though he knew his son had emotional problems, he refused to help me. When I turned to Tommy's mother for help, she made it clear she did not want to hear about the abuse. They did not want to deal with Tommy's emotional problems when he was a child and they were not about to face it once he was married. Neighbors of theirs have told me that Tommy had this problem with his "temper" (a clever name for insanity) throughout childhood and that his parents continually handled it with denial. Years later my ex-husband moved back in with his parents and, guess what? His violence became their problem once again. Sow and reap. Sow and reap.

Forgiveness allows the victim to put her energy into becoming healthy and strong rather than seeking vengeance. Enough of her time and well-being has been sacrificed on his insanity. Besides, creating a successful life is the best revenge.

STEP SEVEN

Now that your self-esteem is becoming your own and getting stronger, it is very important to move to step seven and set some realistic goals for yourself. What do you want to do with your future? What have you always wanted to do or be? Think back to childhood, if you need to, and think about what talents and skills just came naturally to you. How could those evolve into a profession?

When I was a young girl, I was the person my family and friends came to with their problems. I was always attempting to fix other peoples' problems. So it only makes sense I went into the field of psychology, and I thrive in it. Think about your own natural gifts and talents. Where could they be best used? Do you have an interest in the healing of the physical body? Perhaps nursing or another occupation in the medical field would be right for you. Are you creative and drawn to fixing your friend's hair? Cosmetology school may be for you. Do you find the law to be interesting? That may be your avenue to pursue.

You can go to any local college and ask a career counselor to help you with this decision about your future. There are computerized tests that can determine which occupations are best suited for your personality. There should be little or no charge for this service. Take that first step and go talk to someone at the college. Many colleges have a Women's Center and they specialize in "transitional careers" for women. If you have not finished high school, they can help you to get a GED. If college is not for you, they can still point you in the right direction for whatever it is you would like to do.

It is not fair but reality is that you will probably need to be the primary provider for yourself and your children. Most abusive men make lousy fathers and are not diligent in paying child support. It is not fair, but it often happens. So you need to determine what you are going to do with your life. The good news is working towards your goals and achieving them will be very fulfilling and will do wonders for your self-esteem. It is a wonderful feeling when you realize you are no longer dependent on child support from your abusive partner to survive.

Your goal may or may not require schooling. If it does, go again to the women's center or financial aid office at your local college and find out about scholarships and grants available to women returning to school with children. Scholarships and grants do not have to be paid back. There is an abundance of money out there for tuition and cost of living if you are willing to go out and search for it. Try the library. There are books on what scholarships and grants are available. Apply to every one that you can. Filling out the paperwork is definitely a hassle but the payoff is well worth the time spent. The Internet may also have many listings for scholarships.

I applied for countless scholarships. Some came through

and some did not. When they did, a few hundred dollars here and there helped tremendously while going to school and raising children. One semester I began receiving an extra $200.00 check each month. When I called the administrator about it, he said it was an error that they were going to let slide. He said to enjoy the semester! I was thrilled. You just never know what is going to happen in life. That extra money made my life much easier during that time period.

But no one is going to just hand it to you. You will have to be willing to go out and find the opportunities. Many wealthy people or corporations believe in the value of education and have set up scholarships for people who cannot afford it on their own. It is a way for them to help others while providing a tax break for themselves. Take advantage of these scholarships and make your life better. It is a good feeling to receive financial aid from people who believe that you are worthy of getting an education. And you are!

SUMMARY

Believe in your worth. It is time to be your own best friend and learn how to genuinely like and respect yourself. It is possible to have a healthy sense of self, regardless of what circumstances you have experienced. Giving thought and energy to yourself can create a healthy self-esteem. You deserve it. After all, you are a Worthy Woman.

This is your time to get your life back on track. You had the incredible strength and intelligence to survive and escape from a violent marriage. Now take that same strength within you and put it into creating a career for yourself. That career will enable you and your children to have a good life independent of whether or not a child support check is in the mail. Your self-esteem is in your hands now; make it what you want. This is your time to make yourself a Worthy Woman, and no one can stop you unless you let him or her.

The Abuser

Chapter Ten: Why?

Let me begin this section with an apology. I am so sorry that many women do not know that there are good, kind men in the world. I am also sorry that it is necessary to refer to the abuser as "he." My apology goes out to all the kind, loving men who treat their wives and children with the respect they deserve. And even more so to all the men who are the victims in abusive relationships.

But the fact remains that more than 95 percent of abuse is done by a male to a female. Many women have given up hope that kind men do, indeed, exist. But they do. Many men have learned in childhood or adulthood that kindness is the key to a healthy relationship. They know that the appropriate way to treat a woman is with respect. Kindness and integrity are the standard in normal, healthy relationships. This is not a fantasy; these types of relationships do exist. I know because I am finally in one with my husband. And most of our friends have the same high standards of interpersonal relating in their marriages.

WHY DO MEN ABUSE THEIR PARTNERS?
This is a multifaceted question with many different answers. Abuse is always about one person attempting to control another, but that does not address the question of "why." Listed below are some of the factors, which help to explain why the abuser chooses this outlet for his emotions.

CHILDHOOD TRAINING
Violence is accepted as normal male behavior in much of this country. Our group consciousness accepts that aggression is an acceptable, normal part of the male species. Turn on a television any night of the week or go to a movie and you will see evidence of this. Little boys and little girls are conditioned differently when they are growing up. When girls get in a physical fight, they are stopped and expected to resolve their conflicts in a peaceful, quiet, verbal manner. When boys get in a fight they are allowed to duke it out. Verbalizing feelings is not viewed as a "guy" thing to do. The stronger child is given respect for his strength by his peers and adults. The "wimp" is looked down upon.

Little boys learn early on that brute force is something admired at some level by the majority of people in our society. Children's behavior is strongly impacted by attention and approval. They will increase the behavior which gives them extra emotional strokes. They will decrease the behaviors that do not. Boys are not given as much approval for talking about their feelings as for acting them out physically. As a whole, we are giving our little boys attention for being bullies. Men do not want their sons to be the "wimp" and, truthfully, neither do mothers.

Fortunately for some boys, they are given another message that overrides this one. They are taught males and females are to be treated with respect. They have learned that talking out feelings is a good thing and it shows strength of character.

These boys learn from the adults in their lives that relationships are not about control but about mutual respect. The most powerful influence on children is what takes place in their home. Parents have more of an impact on their children than society. Many children grow up to be nonviolent adults because of their upbringing in spite of the violence in our culture.

Children learn what they live. If children are raised with emotional, physical, verbal and/or sexual abuse in their home, they will probably end up being adults who abuse or who are abused. Children learn how to respond by watching those around them. Many children learn that the way to survive life is by using physical force, that it is good to have power over another. Unfortunately, power and control are reinforced in every aspect of our media. Most movies geared towards children have violence in them.

Every abusive man I have seen in therapy came from a background where some form of abuse was taking place. Abuse can come in many forms such as verbal, emotional or physical. There may be exceptions to this but, more times than not, an abuser was abused in some way as a child. A child watching as the mother gets beaten is experiencing emotional child abuse. That child is as much a victim as the woman.

Abusive men did not learn that the best way to survive life is with peace and integrity. Respect in a relationship is foreign to them. They learned that relationships are about controlling the other person. Yelling is the norm, talking out emotions is not within their behavioral repertoire. No one taught them what is and is not appropriate behavior in a relationship. They learned to come out swinging.

UNCONTROLLED ANGER

Children need to learn internal boundaries for their anger. Most children go through a period of temper tantrums when they are under age five and then, again, when they are in their teens. It is the parents' responsibility at those times to teach them to develop internal boundaries on their angry behavior. The parents need to do this through nonviolent, consistent discipline, which will be discussed in the last chapter. It is easier to let a child have a temper tantrum, than to stop it by taking the time to discipline appropriately; but that is a parent's job. Not doing it is just lazy parenting and damaging for the child.

An abuser continues to have uncontrolled, childlike temper tantrums in adulthood because he did not learn to internally control anger in childhood. Over half the children in our society end up being raised in a single parent home by their mothers at some point in their lives. Having been a single parent for most of my children's lives, I know how difficult it is to be both father and mother. It is hard to have the strength to be a firm disciplinarian on our own. But we have no choice if we want to parent effectively.

Our children need discipline just as much as they need love. The ideal is for fathers to be fathers and to discipline their children appropriately. But because of how we have socialized men, mothers have to learn to toughen up and attempt to be both father and mother. Isn't that an enabling reaction? Perhaps, but realistically, someone has to love and discipline the children. If the fathers cannot, will not or are not capable, the kids cannot be sacrificed.

I complimented one of my clients the other day on his involvement as a parent with his young children. I told him what an excellent father I thought he was. His response was so appropriate. He said, "No, I am just being a father. The problem is that most men are not." This sums up one of the major crisis in our society. Men are not being fathers to their children and the children desperately need fathers.

THE PROBLEM SOLVER

Men are taught from a young age that their role in a relationship is to be the problem solver. If an issue comes up, the man feels a responsibility to create the solution. If he does not, then he deems himself a failure. There is an attitude in our society that men are supposed to be Prince Charming with all the answers. This is a frustrating role for men in general because it is not humanly possible to have the right answer for everyone all the time, or even half of the time.

For an abuser the pressure to be the problem solver is overwhelming. Consequently, any minor issue can trigger an intense emotion because they are already at the stressed-out point. For them, it is like living in a pressure cooker. The pressure of the internal belief of the male's responsibility is just too much. When he cannot come up with an answer, the feelings of being a failure add to an already existing poor self-esteem. Even if the woman says she is not looking for a solution to an issue, it doesn't matter. It is his job! These internalized beliefs were developed somewhere along the way in childhood. We all have untrue beliefs that we have to recognize and change from childhood, its just part of life. As adults we need to overcome these irrational childhood beliefs.

ABORTED ADULT EMOTIONAL DEVELOPMENT

Abusers have not yet reached the adult stage of emotional development. Adulthood is when most normal people assume responsibility for their own behavior in spite of what happened to them in childhood or at any other time in their lives. We choose to live a principled life based on an internalized base of integrity. We value ourselves and other people and treat them with respect. Thought is put into our words and our actions. We think before we speak and act. We learn to control our impulses and evaluate what choice is best.

Our tolerance broadens and we learn not to "sweat the small

stuff." And then we realize it is all small stuff unless it is life threatening. We prefer to take the high road in decision-making. Some people do not reach this stage of adulthood, especially abusers. Abusers got "stuck" emotionally at a young age with poor impulse control and little tolerance for stress. Life is not easy for them or for anyone living with them. Stress is a normal part of life, but abusers have not developed coping skills for stress and working it through. Their response to this emotion is to explode.

INSECURITIES

Insecurities can cause people to be self-consumed and blind to other feelings. A self-consumed person has little regard or compassion for other people. Their insecure feelings force them to stay focused on themselves and their own perceived unmet needs. They develop narcissistic beliefs that they are entitled to special treatment because their feelings are all that matter. Abusers do not have much empathy for others because they are so caught up in their own emotional pain. People are to be used as objects to help them to feel better. In psychology it is called "object love." Every abused woman knows what it is like to be loved like an object rather than a human being with feelings.

By the way, it is the pain caused by insecurities the codependent partner senses and wants to "fix". But no one can fix the insecurities but the insecure person. He has to choose to change, but if brute force keeps his insecurities protected, why would he change? The insecurities are the reason abusers have such a need to control. They do not trust the world and they believe they have to control it. So they use what has worked in the past, and that is abusive behavior. The abuser is afraid of what his world would be like if he was not in control. But this thinking is delusional because he is not in control anyway, not really.

132

The abuser is afraid to be rejected yet he sets himself up for it by using abusive behavior towards those he wants near him. The belief is that to avoid rejection (his greatest fear), he must force and control people who need and love him. However, control and love do not mix, and so the cycle escalates. The more he abuses, the more he ends up being rejected. This just confirms his belief that people are not to be trusted. He may never learn that his control is damaging his life and creating what he fears most. The more the victim withdraws emotionally and physically because of the abuse, the more he escalates the control; it's the only response he knows.

DENIAL

Abusers live in a world of denial. I laugh to myself whenever I think of my daughter's response when I asked her what she thought her father's reaction to this book would be. She replied that he'd say, "Who is this Tommy guy? Has he hurt you? Do I need to take care of him?" Every woman who has been in an abusive relationship can appreciate the humor and the sadness of this story.

Most of the abusive men I have seen in therapy deny they have been abusive. They excuse their actions by putting the blame on the victim and by minimizing their act of violence. They genuinely believe the violence was justified and that it was not a big deal. It is not their fault. Unfortunately, most of the victims will contribute to this denial by blaming themselves in some way for the abuse. But there is no excuse for abuse. If the victim wrongly assumes responsibility for it, she is enhancing his denial, which damages everyone.

With the small percent of abusive men who do stick it out in therapy, it is an amazing process to observe as they begin to face the reality of their abusive actions. Once the shield of denial is slowly removed they are shocked by how adamantly they had been excusing the abuse. It is like they have been wearing mental blinders that are suddenly removed.

ONE HUNDRED PERCENT RESPONSIBILITY

To get out of denial the abuser must assume one hundred percent of the responsibility for his violence. No other percentage works. It has to be one hundred percent or they are still in denial. The victim must overcome her denial and develop a zero tolerance for abuse. Zero, no more.

Recently I asked a group of women at a shelter why they thought their partners were abusive. Most of the women have lived with the abuser for at least four years and have children with him. The violence has occurred throughout the relationships, increasing in intensity and frequency. Their answers are listed below. It is evident that some women are also in denial and blaming themselves for the abuse, while others have become healthier and are looking for answers within the abuser.

"I gave him too much control by being submissive."

"I nagged him."

"My husband would slap me when I made him angry."

"I made him mad. I should have kept my mouth shut."

"I don't know what I did wrong. He stabbed me with a butcher knife twice."

"He was an older man that found me, a young lady separated from her parents. He found my weakness."

"He is mentally ill and a drug abuser."

"I made three times his salary so he was jealous. It was his way of thinking he was in control, 'the man.'"

"Guilt over his infidelity."

"He has low self esteem."

"He is unsure of himself. He is angry about his past. He has not dealt with his issues. He is not honest about his life."

"He is really insecure about himself. He doesn't love himself and he doesn't know how to love."

"He wanted to control me. He has so much hate inside him and he seems to need to take it out on someone. He thinks it is okay to treat your wife that way."

One of the women had a broken arm and had just undergone facial reconstructive surgery due to the last episode of abuse. She has permanently lost part of her vision. Still she is in denial about his need to accept the responsibility for the abuse. She blames herself. Although living at a shelter, she sneaks out to meet with him on a regular basis. She is afraid to face the reality of leaving him and being alone with her children. She wants to believe that he will change. I understand her feelings. Most women who have been abused have gone through this period of denial and fear.

The director of the shelter said the woman is beginning to make some progress. At least she will now admit that he is the one who did this to her. In the past, she blamed all of the physical damage on accidents. To stop this terrible assault on women, the men must assume one hundred percent responsibility and the women must develop zero tolerance for the abuse. Denial must be a thing of the past.

SUMMARY

These are some of the many reasons as to why men abuse their partners. They make sense. We can understand how the abusive behavior has developed. Many abusers are victims of society and of their childhood homes. They have been encouraged to be verbally and physically aggressive in relationships in subtle or not so subtle ways. But no matter how much we analyze the background of the violence, the fact remains that an abuser must assume responsibility for his violent choices.

Now, I know how codependent victims think. They start feeling sorry for the abuser when they look at the reasons why he developed abusive behavior. It is sad that he was not conditioned differently. But as an adult, his choices are his responsibility. And abusers need to be treated like adults, not children. We all have issues from childhood we need to overcome in adulthood. Reasons do not justify abusive behavior towards another person. There are services and programs to help him change if he really wants to but the victim cannot be his therapist. Abuse is never okay.

Chapter Eleven: Stopping the Violence

This chapter is devoted to the abuser. Why? Because much to my surprise, I have had abusive men read about my story and call for therapy. God bless them. I hope that this chapter speaks to them.

"JOHN"

"John" told me he knew he was going to lose his wife if he did not get rid of his "temper." She had already filed for divorce, a time when abusers typically re-think their patterns. He said after reading my story he could tell I was not a man-hater and that I believed in marriage. John wanted me to work with him in therapy because he thought I would understand. He was right and we worked hard to overcome his violent tendencies. It was painful and difficult for him to face what he had done and where the violence had begun. Even though it was difficult, he came to his weekly therapy appointments faithfully and worked through his abuse issues. Unfortunately, it was too late and too much damage had occurred for the marriage to survive. His wife could not let herself trust him again. The divorce was inevitable. But still, he was a changed man.

STEPS FOR SEEKING HELP

What can be done to help abusers overcome this violent behavior that is part of who they are? There is definitely help for the abuser, but he has to be the one to choose to get it. The victim cannot do it for him. And an abuser will not seek out help as long as he is in denial unless he is forced to by circumstances. Listed below are some of the steps needed for the abusive person to overcome his terrible problem.

A. The victim must stop denying or downplaying the violence. This is the one thing the victim can do to help the abuser. She must stop assuming any responsibility for the abuse. The abuser is in enough denial himself; he does not need anyone else, especially the victim, doing it for him. The victim must speak the truth calmly and realistically about what is happening in the relationship not just to the abuser, but also to other family members who are involved. Even if everyone in the extended family and friends wants to stay in denial, the victim needs to be speaking the truth about the abuse. Being based in reality is the only hope for good mental health. Passively accepting the abuse is not good for anyone involved. It is just fuel for the already existing smoldering flames of anger. Being based in reality is the only path to good mental health. Denial just distorts reality.

Of course, once the victim gets out of denial and starts speaking the truth, there is a risk that the violence will increase in an attempt to control her. She has to make a plan to keep herself and the children safe if this should happen. Yet an abuser typically does not get help for himself until his partner has faced reality and is leaving him, has left him or until he is in trouble with the law. Let me repeat, this can also be the time when some men become the most violent so the victim needs to have her safety plan in effect.

B. The abuser must engage in outside help. Some domestic violence shelters have ongoing therapy for the abusers. If the local shelters do not, then they will know where the abuser can go to get quality counseling. People working at shelters tend to be experts in the area of domestic violence. They know and understand what is going on out there. They can determine which techniques are the best for working through the violent problems. The therapy at the shelters may be in groups or individual. After speaking to the abuser the shelter can determine what type of treatment would be the most effective.

Many counties now court order abusers to attend counseling when they are brought before the judge on domestic violence charges. Although the men are reluctant to attend the counseling sessions initially, many of them end up learning a great deal about themselves. Some begin to develop anger management skills. The men learn what is and is not appropriate, normal behavior in relationships with their spouse and children. Many abusers are surprised to realize how abnormal and damaging their "normal" behavior was. The court-ordered therapy is long term, meaning that it lasts for months or years.

C. The abuser can seek out private therapy. Some men decide they would rather seek out private counseling than have their partner leave them, so they contact a therapist before there are any legal issues. The most important factor in selecting a therapist is knowing that he or she has experience with domestic violence issues or anger management training. Not all credentialed therapists are familiar with spousal abuse. This would be an important question to ask the therapist before making an appointment. If they do not have the experience, call another one. It may be helpful to contact a counselor who specializes in marriage and family counseling.

Referrals from friends or family members that have had effective therapy can be a good resource. Most therapists in private practice charge a high fee but the majority of it may be covered by health insurance. The cost is an investment in the abuser's marriage and future. A good therapist is worth his or her weight in gold. What price can be put on a changed life? I might be biased about that, but I have had the privilege of seeing hundreds of people's lives turn around through weekly, long-term therapy. Psychotherapy works for most people.

D. The person who has been abusive cannot overcome the violence problem on his own. Trying to overcome violent tendencies alone is like an addict trying to get sober without help. Rarely can they succeed without outside intervention. Most habitual behavior can be stopped for about 21 days before the person repeats it. Most addicts can maintain sobriety about that long on their own without help. It is the same length of time with abusers controlling their urges. The tendency towards violence is a deeply imprinted habitual pattern within the psyche that needs to be replaced with more appropriate behaviors.

It is impossible to be objective or resourceful enough to work this through alone. And the abuser cannot do it with his spouse. She cannot be objective on this issue and needs her own help. A third party needs to intervene. Seeking counseling is a humbling act of admitting the need for help. Yet it is such a healthy step towards growth. Life is tough and sometimes we need help. In a perfect world we would all have the skills to make it though life effectively. That is rarely the case. We need to seek out direction at times by discussing our issues with someone. The Bible says to "share your burdens, one to another" (Gal 6:2). Isn't that great? God put that in there because He knew we would need to do just that periodically to make it through life effectively.

Sometimes men need help in spite of the pervasive myth that men are to be the ultimate problem solvers. It is not possible for anyone to have all the answers about everything. I have found that most men really enjoy the process of therapy once they let their protective guard down. It is a relief to be able to problem solve with another person rather than carrying the burden alone. Identifying and verbalizing feelings help in reducing stress.

E. Persistence and patience are crucial for healing. There is no quick fix. Anger issues are not overcome within a few sessions with a therapist. It takes months and months of hard work and regular appointments to begin to change the violent behavior patterns. Going to a therapist three or four times is not magically going to cure anything; especially the controlling, angry behavior of abuse.

We are a society that wants immediate gratification, but that is not realistic when it comes to making changes in our psychological makeup. It takes time and effort for genuine change to take place. There is no pill to make it all better. Therapy is like pumping iron; it takes a long time to get the results you desire, but it is well worth the effort. Learning to delay gratification by working hard on a problem for an extended period of time to get the desired results is a form of maturity.

It is very important for the victim to also recognize that the abuser is not going to change with just a couple of visits to the shrink. Victims have the tendency to grab on to any glimmer of hope to save the relationship. Many women have been fooled into trusting there would be no more violence because of a few therapy sessions only to be brutalized once again. Remember, most people can stop a habitual behavior pattern for about 21 days; then the damaging behavior may return in full force.

F. Abusers need to develop a spiritual base of integrity. A strong moral ethic of what is right and wrong needs to be developed at the internal core of the person's decision-making base. When this occurs, the person can make behavioral choices based on integrity rather than on impulsive, angry emotions. This spiritual maturity takes time and persistence to develop. Incorporating moral ethics into our lives usually involves developing a relationship with God (or a Higher Power).

Although God is quite capable of healing a person's emotions instantaneously, He usually does not. We have been given the ability to overcome our own psychological issues with hard work and effort. Many abusive men who suddenly get "religion" continue to be violent. Unfortunately, some religious men are also abusers. They are control freaks and can misinterpret what the Bible says about women to justify abusive behavior.

Sometimes women believe that the abuse is over once their partner starts talking about God. Talking about spiritual issues is great but it takes effort and time before a person is able to, as Alcoholics Anonymous says, "walk their talk." I love that phrase "walk your talk" because that is one of the keys to good mental health. Just giving lip service to living with integrity is very easy, living it is another issue.

God has provided us with the field of psychology to help us with life. Remember the advice I got from my minister was that I needed to harden myself and accept the abuse because divorce was not acceptable. He pointed out to me a broken down woman in the church who had been in a violent marriage for more than thirty years. As if that were virtuous. Boy, was he off the mark. God hates cruel men (Malachi 2:16). Some churches provide good counseling but it is important to make sure that the counselors have graduate training in therapy. Domestic violence is not a simple issue to work through.

There may be other ways for an abuser to get help and to overcome his violent tendencies. Each person should seek out what methods feel right for him or her. Developing a moral base of integrity is a necessary tool in the healing process. The key issue here is taking the first step to seek out some kind of help for change and sticking with it for the long haul. It is highly unlikely the abuser is going to become nonviolent on his own.

G. The abuser must assume one hundred percent responsibility for the violence. One hundred percent of the responsibility by the abuser and zero tolerance of the abuse by the victim. This is the most difficult yet healing step in the processing of change. The abuser must stop blaming anyone or anything else for the abuse. It is his, he must own it. No one made him abuse and no one can prevent him from doing it again, except himself. It is true that the abusive behavior was probably learned somewhere in childhood, but that does not excuse it. As adults we have freedom to choose how we are going to behave. We do not have to stay stuck in what we learned in childhood. Thank God.

SUMMARY

Change cannot truly occur unless the man accepts total responsibility for his violent tendencies. It is a painful thing to do, but it also freeing. That is the point where the abuser takes control over the violence rather than the rage taking control of him. He can learn how to live life without the pain of his insecurities. He can learn how to have genuine joy and happiness. When that happens, there is no need to control people. Violence becomes a thing of the past.

Abusers can learn how to love. If you have ever been physically rough or verbally mean towards your wife or children, please get help. The greatest strength of character a man can develop is the ability to be gentle. Gentlemen are the strongest men of all. You can learn how to be in a mutually gratifying love relationship which is really what you want most of all. It will be a relationship based on peace, not war. And it will feel good.

Patience is another virtue that you will need to develop. If your spouse stays with you, it will take time for her to learn to trust your new behavior; at least a year. Be patient as you continue to work on your own growth. You have not been a safe person for her. The trust that was once so freely given now has to be earned back. The Bible says, in the first chapter of James, that you can learn to be complete, lacking nothing, if you learn how to be patient.

There is an added bonus to learning how to love a woman appropriately with kindness. The very nature of women is to be loving towards those who treat us with kindness. That is a very general statement but it is true for most women. We want and need to be treated in a positive way. In turn, we just naturally give positive back to those who are good to us. Not only will it be good for your self-esteem to become a gentleman, you will have a good chance at receiving healthy love from a woman. When people feel safe, they can be vulnerable to love. Make her safe and she will love you.

May God bless you as you overcome your violent tendencies. God wants you to replace your inner turmoil with peace and the turmoil in your home with love. Life will be so much better for you.

The Children

Chapter Twelve: Unprotected Victims

What is happening to our children? Who is protecting them from the horrors of domestic violence? Several million children witness domestic violence each year. Not hundreds, but millions of children are learning by watching their parents that violence is a way of life. And we wonder why violence is overtaking our society. There is no getting around the fact that children learn what they live. Violence is being taught to these children right in their homes. Where are their protectors? These child witnesses appear to be an overlooked group of victims in our society. If we want to save our society, we must stand up and assume responsibility for these young victims.

Every child in an abusive home suffers emotional damage caused by the violence. Every child in a violent home is a victim. Children may respond differently to the violence yet psychological damage is done to every one of them. They are all learning by observation that violence is a way of life. They are learning to be the abuser, the victim or both. The damage is easy to see in the aggressive child and much more subtle, in the passive one. Yet the negative impact affects all of the children.

Children need their home to be a safe haven, not a war zone. They need sane adult role models in order to develop psychologically and emotionally. Quite simply, the way to help these unprotected victims to develop good mental health is by ending their exposure to the violence. Parents must stop the violence in the home or get out and create a peaceful home for the children. Parents must assume the responsibility of being the protectors of their own children.

Programs to help the children of domestic violence are just beginning to be established throughout the country in shelters. Putting the children in a mental health program can be very beneficial, but they should not continue to be exposed to the violence. Mental health programs cannot override the emotional damage that is being created in the violent home. The programs create an environment where it is safe for children to talk about feelings associated with what they have witnessed. A violent home is not normal and it is not a safe place to open up emotionally. The overwhelming feelings of fear and helplessness need to be talked about. Kids need to know that the violence is not their fault. If those feelings are held in, depression, anxiety and rage are sure to manifest at some time in the child's life.

Recently I spoke at a shelter and asked the woman how many children they had and their ages. Most had at least two children and the age range was from infancy to adulthood. These are children who have seen their mothers hit, shoved, stabbed, choked, thrown into walls and worse. Many had learned to react to the violence by becoming violent or by shrinking inwardly with fear. The children's reactions are normal in an abnormal home. It is difficult to stay sane in an insane situation.

One of the women made a statement that made me cringe. She said, "My boy is growing up to be a bully just like his father." God help that child. Where do you think he learned this behavior? This child needs to be taught healthy ways to express his emotions. Who is going to teach him if his mother already labels him as "being like his father" and his father is violent? Children from violent homes need to be taught there is another way to behave that feels so much better than being aggressive. They need to be retaught what is and is not appropriate behavior and how to resolve conflicts without violence.

POST TRAUMATIC STRESS

Many of these unprotected children experience stress symptoms similar to those exhibited by war veterans. Some of the symptoms of Post Traumatic Stress Syndrome in children are agitation, irritability, anger, mistrust, paranoia, nightmares, reenacting of the violence in play and a short attention span. Trouble in school is common either with acting out behavior or lack of concentration. The children are preoccupied with worry for themselves and their parents. It is a burden children should not be forced to carry. Yet if they are in a violent home, they cannot help but be psychologically weighed down with fear and helplessness.

It is so sad to see the fear within the eyes of the children. Whether they develop a defense of being tough with an attitude or withdrawing into themselves, they are both based in fear. These kids are afraid and rightfully so. The defenses they use are survival techniques subconsciously employed to be able to cope emotionally with the hostile environment they live in and have no choice. In a healthy home, parents are protectors of the children. In an unhealthy home, the children feel a need to fear and/or protect their parents. Something is very wrong when innocent children must shoulder such a heavy burden.

These children have learned that the world at large is neither trustworthy nor safe. If their parents represent the world and they are not to be trusted emotionally, then people in general are not worthy of trust. They learn that fathers, who represent all men, are to be feared because they are out of control and violent. And mothers are not safe either because they allow themselves to be abused. If the women cannot protect themselves, how can the children trust them to be their protector? If children do not get emotional security from home, they will find it elsewhere. Children need to feel like they belong to a safe group of people. If it is not the family, then whatever is available will take its place.

EFFECTS OF ABUSE AT ALL STAGES

Children of all ages are affected by the violence in their homes. Unfortunately there is a myth that small children are not affected by what they are exposed to at home. This could not be farther from the truth. Children are forming their basic personalities from birth to age five. These personalities will last them a lifetime. Changing what is learned during this time period is a challenging task. Defenses and inappropriate behaviors learned in childhood are difficult to overcome in adulthood. It is one of the main issues of psychotherapy and it takes much hard work on the client's part to change childhood survival defense patterns.

INFANTS

Many women who have been physically abused while pregnant have infants with colic. The theory is that these babies have felt the anxiety from their mother's body while in the womb. Every cell of our bodies reacts to each motion we feel. Consequently, the stress within the woman's body is transferred onto the baby's still developing little body. The intense crying is a reflection of the lack of peace and ease in the infant's body. Ideally, pregnancy should be a time of peace for the mother and the developing baby.

TODDLERS

Toddlers through age five show signs of being whining and clingy or overly aggressive towards others when exposed to abuse in the home. Years ago when I taught preschool it was easy to determine which aggressive behaviors children were learning in their homes. Clearly some of them were witnessing physical abuse. They were coming in and acting out what they had learned by watching their parents. They would reenact the violence in their play behavior because they learned people relate to one another through violence. The other children would avoid them or become victims of the aggression. Violence is the only way some children know how to control or relate to the world. Other preschoolers from violent homes would be fearful and clingy because they had learned that their world was not safe.

PREADOLESCENCE

Preadolescent children from violent homes may react in a variety of ways. Some children continue to exhibit the aggressive behavior and others become depressed and fearful. Low self-esteem is an ongoing issue for all these children because somewhere within themselves they think the violence is their fault. Children are egocentric out of necessity for survival. They blame themselves for problems in the home. This is the origin of shame. It is difficult for them to step outside themselves and realize that the violence is not their fault. The internal belief is that they deserve what they are getting in the home although there is no rhyme or reason to it. Some children become socially isolated because they fear bringing friends into their hostile environment. They are embarrassed when they realize their home is different than their friends.

149

TEENS

Adolescents, especially boys, from violent homes are more prone than other teens to delinquency and physical assaults. This is especially true if they have spent many years in a violent home. Some of the teen boys and girls choose to escape through substance abuse in an attempt to dull their painful feelings. This is a very dangerous path. Suicide is another avenue the depressed adolescent may consider for escape. The number of teen suicides increases each year. Sexual acting out is common as an attempt to feel close and comforted, unlike what they feel at home.

While some of the teens are outwardly acting out their emotions in unhealthy ways, equally as damaging are the teens that stay at home trying to be responsible and put sanity into the insane environment. They do not have the power to control the violence, but they desperately try. Assuming responsibility for the damaged home is an unrealistic and overwhelming task. These teens repress their emotions until the day comes when they are ready to explode with anxiety or depression. Some teens may assume parenting roles for the younger siblings while ignoring their own unmet needs. At some point these codependents will need to work on their own damaged emotions. They take care of everyone else, but who is taking care of them?

NOT A PRETTY PICTURE

The victimization of the children is not a pretty picture. Unfortunately, it is a picture that not many people are looking at. As a society we need to be looking long and hard at what is happening to these children. We have failed the children by allowing domestic violence to become acceptable through the sin of omission. Because we have closed our eyes to domestic abuse, we have taught generations of children that the way to express feelings and to resolve conflict is with violence.

After all, if dad beats mom and mom accepts it, then it must be okay and normal. And if a child is hit, shoved and berated for discipline, he or she learns that the bigger and stronger person gets their way, the angriest person "wins." In a domestic violence situation, the anger level is pervasive in the home. Both parents tend to discipline with physical and mental abuse rather then with education because everyone is on the edge. Dad has little impulse control and Mom feels like her nerves cannot take any more stress. Everyone is out of control, so who is teaching the children about being an emotionally disciplined person?

We must learn to discipline our children in a controlled, peaceful fashion rather than through aggression. They need to feel safe in their environment. Angry parents who impulsively lash out physically or verbally are not safe. It is in the presence of peace that people become energized and centered. This enables us to go out and deal with the many challenging issues in life in a healthy way without stressing out with anxiety and depression.

Anxiety and depression are breeding grounds for rage and inappropriate behavior. We no longer have the luxury of disciplining our children anyway we want. Consistent, educative, disciplined discipline in a peaceful home is the only way to raise children to be healthy, nonviolent individuals. This technique for discipline will be discussed in detail in the next chapter. Children learn how to deal with life by watching what is taking place in the home. And violence is taking place in one form or another in over half of our homes. Millions of children are being affected.

SUMMARY

Why are we so surprised by the violence now being exhibited by the children on the streets? And it is going to get worse if we do not take a stand for peace in our homes. We simply must take a stand against violence for our children and our children's children. We must teach our children how to respect themselves and others. They need to know that physical abuse is never okay.

"We are called to peace" (ICor7: 15). Within every one of us is a need, not just a desire but also a need, for peace. We need peace as much as we need water and air to survive in an effective way. Our homes should be a refuge for our children. The home should be a peaceful place to come to get emotionally fueled up. As parents it is our responsibility to create this kind of environment. Loving, stable discipline is the key to a peaceful home. If our homes are not a place of peace, then it is time to get busy in order to make changes.

While I was still married, the scripture verse about peace became so clear to me during a time of prayer. I knew that the ideal was to keep my children in a two-parent home and stay married. But the reality was that my spouse was violent and above all, I needed to get my children and myself into a home of peace. If we were going to be mentally healthy people, we could not live under the dark cloud of violence. We had to have a home that would be a refuge of peace. This is one of the primary factors that enabled me to muster up the enormous courage required to leave my abusive spouse. Once I got out and began the awesome task of single parenting, I quickly had to learn how to discipline in a disciplined manner so that there would not be violence in our home. We all had our fill of that.

The next chapter is dedicated to a basic four step method of disciplining children in a disciplined manner. Any parent can put this four step method into practice. It is a giant step in establishing a peaceful household with your children once you have removed yourself from the violence. Peace can prevail.

Chapter Thirteen: Disciplined Discipline

Parenting is an awesome responsibility, and being a single parent is even more challenging. But it certainly is possible to raise children effectively alone. Of course the ideal is to have a two-parent peaceful home but, unfortunately, that is not the reality in a domestic violence situation. Children do much better in a single parent peaceful home than in a two-parent violent one.

I have found that disciplined discipline is the key to having a peaceful home with children. It takes controlled effort and energy to do a good job in the area of discipline. This chapter will describe an effective four step method of disciplining children without violence and with respect.

After my children were born I spent a great deal of time thinking about this new experience of parenting. What was the best way to raise children? God bless my parents, but I knew I wanted to do a better job of parenting than they did. So I began to pray that God would reveal to me how to parent these babies I loved so much.

Interestingly enough, within a few weeks a friend came over with a brochure on parenting that she had gotten from a church.

It had four steps to disciplining with love listed in detail with scriptural backing. As soon as I read it, it became alive to me. I knew that this little booklet was the truth for me about how to parent effectively. From that day forward I used these four steps to raise my children. It is a method that can be used effectively by mothers as well as fathers. Men typically have an easier time getting children to mind than women but this technique is equally effective for both parents.

As I became a psychologist, I found that from a psychological perspective the method was right on the mark. I have now used this four step method with hundreds of families in therapy and family groups and have found it to be extremely effective. I have modified the steps from the booklet through the years to eliminate any type of physical punishment, but the concepts are basically the same. This method is a nonviolent way of disciplining children with respect for the parents and for them.

FOUR STEPS TO EFFECTIVE PARENTING
STEP ONE: EXPECTATIONS

Determine what you expect from each child. What do you expect each child to do or not do? Are your expectations age appropriate? Sit down with a sheet of paper and make a list of your expectations for each child. Discuss them with people whom you believe are knowledgeable about children and get their opinion. Go to the library and look up books on child development to learn what children are capable of at different ages. Parenting is a job to be taken very seriously and requires researching various topics at times. Keep in mind; this is the most important job you will ever have. It is easy to expect too much or too little from our children. You have to take into account the developmental level and personality of your child as well as their age.

One child at twelve may be capable of much more than

another child of that same age. Do not expect your child to be like your friend's child or sibling's child. Each child is unique with his or her own set of abilities. Once you have compiled your list and checked it, then it is time to sit down with your child and discuss the list in detail. Children of all ages need to be told things in detail so you both have a clear understanding of what is expected. Trust me, your concept of a clean room is very different than your child's. If having a clean room is one of the expectations, then list every item included to eliminate confusion or miscommunication. Do this with every item on the list.

Have your child repeat back to you what is on the list so you are both very clear on the expectations. Be open to discussing any concerns your child may have. Our children may have valid points to make in any decision making process involving them. They deserve the respect of you listening to their opinions. But, remember, it is for their benefit when you insist that they be responsible at home. A learned sense of responsibility will transfer into their everyday lives. It will help them respect themselves and others.

TWO TABOOS

One realistic expectation that should be an ongoing rule in your home is that there is to be NO physical violence or name calling between siblings. Yes, sibling rivalry is normal but it should not be allowed to include anything physical or degrading. It is our responsibility as parents to prevent this from occurring. There is nothing "normal" about allowing physical harm or mental humiliation to take place with our children. Those behaviors are just another form of domestic violence. Allowing it is creating a breeding ground for an abuser and a victim. Name-calling and physical fighting is damaging and is not acceptable.

Children need to learn how to respect each other and how

to talk out their conflicts. This is what will benefit them in life. Physical and mental violence will not. The falsehood that "boys will be boys," therefore, violence is okay, is ridiculous. Do not downplay the significance of this rule in your home. If you do, then you are contributing to the violence problem that exists in our society.

STEP TWO: TYPES OF DISCIPLINE

Any type of discipline used should not be violent or condescending towards your child. The goal is to teach our children how to be happy, effective, appropriate people with a healthy self-esteem. We want our children to respect themselves and others. This takes being firm yet loving while disciplining and shaping our children. Make a list of nonviolent forms of discipline techniques that are age appropriate and time appropriate. Once again, books from the library on discipline are helpful. The goal is to use something that does not take longer than twenty minutes. Listed below are two nonviolent methods of discipline that have proven to be very effective for all ages.

A. Time-out. Time-out is one of the most effective methods of discipline starting at about age two on up. For small children it is very important to find a boring corner in your home away from any stimulation like the television or a window. Children thrive on stimulation and the time-out will only be effective if it is void of that. Put down a small chair facing the corner that you call the "time-out chair." When the child needs to be disciplined, he or she sits in the chair immediately for an amount of minutes equal to their age. Use an egg timer or your oven timer to know when the time is up. Then the punishment is over. Do not force your child to sit there longer than that or it will lose its effectiveness. If the child needs to be held gently, yet firmly, in the chair by the shoulder the first couple of times until getting the idea, it is okay. Being sent to their room for time-out is not effective because there is so much stimulation there.

One of the wonderful things about time-out is that it can be used anywhere. In any restaurant, store, home, church or wherever there is always a corner of a bathroom stall that can be used. Children tend to test the boundaries in public places. Time-out is a good nonviolent, nonhumiliating method of discipline. Don't you just cringe when you see a parent yelling at or hitting a child in public? Humiliation is not a healthy means of discipline. I have been known to address those parents. Is it my business? Yes, someone has to protect our children. As a society, it is all of our business.

Time-out can be used for most ages, but the format changes a bit for the older kids. The time-out becomes one of taking a break for twenty minutes from whatever activity the child is currently engaged in. It is far more effective to take a video game, a television show, a bike or whatever away for twenty minutes than taking it away for a day or two. During the twenty minutes the child is anticipating the return of the activity and is able to recognize that this is a punishment. When an activity is removed for a day or more then the child moves on to other things. Teens can be given time-out from the phone, the car, the computer and whatever else they value, but the time-out should be for a limited period of time.

Grounding for an extended period of time is not very effective and tends to be more of a punishment for the parents than for the child. But time-out from a specific activity can be effective if the activity is to take place within a short period of time, less than a week. A blanket grounding like two weeks tends to lose its effectiveness within the first day. The child acclimates to being home and forgets about it. Or worse yet, sometimes the parent cannot tolerate the grounding for the duration, reneges on the punishment and sends the child off to play. The effectiveness of the discipline is then lost.

B. Chores. At about age four children love helping Mommy clean, but within a couple of years, that all changes. Most normal children dislike chores once they reach a certain age. So chores are perfect to use as a form of discipline. Children need to learn how to be proficient at taking care of things around the house; it will help them as adults. And a bit of hard work is healthy. So using chores as discipline is a good choice. These would be chores in addition to the ones the child is already expected to do as a participating member of the household. Being given an immediate chore to do when acting out can begin to be used at about age seven.

I remember a friend of mine who used this method and was a single parent. She was raising two big healthy teenage boys alone. Without a doubt she had the cleanest kitchen floor I had ever seen. The boys knew that if they were inappropriate, they would be on their hands and knees washing that floor, sometimes with a toothbrush. Bathroom floors, toilets, sinks, all the mirrors in the house, the blinds etc. can be used to clean.

In a home, there is always something that can stand a good cleaning. One of the rules is that if it is not done right then it is to be done until it is done correctly. Typically you want to choose a chore that will take less than one half hour to complete. I saved the big jobs like cleaning the garage or the basement for really big inappropriate behavior. Sometimes just the threat of those would be enough. Certainly if a child gets sent home from school for something, they can spend the day cleaning, big time. I have had parents tell me that they could not possibly get their teens to do the chores. Oh, yes, you can. It is all in the way that you present yourself which is part of the next step.

Discuss the discipline options with your children. You may be surprised to find out they can give you some good ideas that you may not have thought of. Or they may be more than happy to give you some great options for their sisters or brothers. The children should be included in the discussions about this new discipline technique. They need to be fully aware of what is going on. Do not expect them to joyfully embrace it. That would be unrealistic. But they need to know and fully understand the new rules in the house before they are implemented

STEP THREE: DISCIPLINED DISCIPLINE

Decide today, right now that you will never repeat yourself more than two times to your child. Never. You will say something once, twice, three times if you need to, then the punishment comes immediately. If you do it a fourth time or more, you will become angry and you will no longer be able to discipline in a calm manner. You will then be disciplining out of anger, and you will be increasing the tension level within the child and both of you will end up being out of control. This is the point where parents lose control.

When everyone is functioning at a high level of tension, any issue can become one of control and end up in a power struggle. At this point no one wins. The discipline must take place way back when everyone is still calm. This is the key to having control as the parent. The level of calm is lost by the fourth repeat. Try it. Tell your child to do something two or three times versus four or five and see what takes place internally. You adrenaline is pumping by the fourth time and you are probably yelling. Disciplined discipline is very difficult to master in this mental state.

Our goal is to discipline before we are angry. When we are angry we lash out impulsively without control. We say and do things that are not appropriate in child rearing. Then our children learn that the way to deal with conflict is to be angry and impulsively lash out. The lashing out is about control. Remember that domestic violence is always about one person trying to control another through brute force. Look around in our society, that is exactly what is happening with this generation of violent children. They have learned that it is okay to lash out when you are angry. They are trying to control their environment with violence.

Discipline, self control and respect have not been learned. Sadly, the majority of this teaching comes from the home. This is coupled with a society that finds violence to be entertaining in the movies and television. Even the Saturday morning cartoons for children tend to be filled with violence. It is so ridiculous. I have threatened to write many letters to actors who are parents that are making these terribly violent films. What are they thinking? Obviously, they are not. We must guard what our children are being exposed to. Just because a film or television show is popular does not mean that it is healthy or appropriate. Many of the titles alone imply violence and murder. Our children deserve the respect of our protection. Maybe if we stop watching and paying for violence, Hollywood will get a clue.

Now it is time to explain this system to the children. They need to know that from now on you will never repeat yourself more than twice. At first they will not believe you, they will test you to try to get the control back, only then will they accept that this is the way it is. Children are very good manipulators. Stick to your plan; do not change it to accommodate a child's whim. Children need discipline to develop into secure, healthy adults. The most secure children are those whose parents care enough to put forth firm boundaries. This allows them to develop internal boundaries on their own behavior. Internal boundaries are what abusers are lacking. Kids function the best in black and white. Gray makes them insecure. They need to know that you love them enough to put forth the energy to care about their behavior.

I remember one time when my children were about seven

and nine; I had regressed into yelling like I was raised with rather than using this technique. This incident occurred one night in when I was putting the children to bed. Nighttime had always been a special time of prayer and warm fuzzies with the children before they would drift off to la la land. On this night I was yelling about something and the phone was ringing so I left their bedroom and slammed the door. On the phone was a pastor asking me if I could come speak to his congregation on disciplining children! God does have a sense of humor. Of course I said "yes" then got on my knees to reevaluate my own home. The next day I sat down with my children and apologized to them for falling into the yelling mode. Yelling is demeaning to children and is damaging to their self-esteem. Immediately I switched back into this four step method. I can still remember the soft blanket of peace that enveloped our home within a day.

JUST DO IT

Now it is time to "just do it." Put the plan into action. There will be many times when you will not feel like getting up and dealing with the discipline, but it is our job. We have to put forth the energy to just do it. In turn we end up with a peaceful household. Your children will test you about every six months or so. During those times you will need to be consistent. Those periods pass and the peace comes back. If you implement this method at least 80 percent of the time you will have a disciplined home with peace. You will find that this method frees you to have more energy to play with and enjoy your children. You no longer have to waste time on tension and moodiness.

STEP FOUR: UNCONDITIONAL LOVE

You have now told your child something three times and then implemented a punishment that lasts less than thirty minutes. You have made your home and your relationship safe, stable and consistent. When a child feels safe, then he or she is ready and able to respond to love. Now it is time to give your child love. You need to restore the fellowship of love between the two of you. It is important to let your child know the behavior was not acceptable now and will not be in the future either. But your love is a constant. That never changes. It is the behavior that you did not like, not the child. They need to know this. I cannot stress enough how important this step is.

Your child needs your love as much as food and water. Your love is what will give your child a healthy sense of self. It is in this love that respect for self and others develops. Do not ever deny your child your love. Always after the discipline restore the bond between the two of you. It is your job to do this, not the child's.

Do not allow negative tension to linger in the air of your home. That is very damaging to everyone in the home, especially the children. Sometimes children will act like they do not want the love but it's not true. Give it to them anyway. Kiss them and hug them even if they push you away. They will come around. Then the tension is gone and you are all free to enjoy each other and yourselves.

It is extremely important that you restore that bond of love with your child after the discipline. In addition, make sure you give your child four positive comments for every negative one. This is the ratio needed, four to one. It takes four positives to cancel out the negative impact on the sense of self from a critical comment. This is true for adults also. Children need healthy positive strokes from at least one of their parents in order to have a healthy self-esteem.

SUMMARY

When a person has a healthy sense of self, there is no need to mistreat or try to control another person. We want to raise our children to be secure with themselves and to have respect for all people. With this four step method of discipline you are teaching your child how to resolve conflicts quickly while showing respect to all parties involved. Out of control behavior is not part of this process. A "temper" is not tolerated. Children learn to develop internal boundaries on their impulses. Abusive behavior is neither shown nor tolerated.

We love our children and want to enjoy our time of raising them. The goal is to get them to adulthood as happy, secure, peaceful individuals. One parent can do it, and the process can begin at any age for the children. It is never too late to teach our children what behavior is and what is not appropriate. Your children may have been exposed to violence, but it is not too late to teach them a different way of living. Talk openly with them about the positive changes in your lives. Teach them about love, peace and discipline.

If you can change and create a healthy life, so can they. Even if your children are adults, they can still learn how to have a healthy life. You are their main role model. They are going to learn about life by watching you. Teach them about genuine love. It is a love that cares enough to say "no" to unhealthy behavior. Let the days of codependency and abuse be well behind all of you. Let domestic violence be a thing of the past. I did it and so can you.